101 COOL HILARIOUS HISTORIES

About the Illustrator:

Glen Singleton has a hilarious history of his own: he has been creating quirky and comical cartoon creations that kids love for over twenty years on topics as diverse as dinosaurs, gnomes, and amusement-park maps! Glen is an artist and the best-selling illustrator of the Hinkler's *Cool* book series as well as many other well-loved children's classics. Based in Brisbane, Australia, one of Glen's particular talents is in creating amazing Australian animal illustrations.

About the Author:

Steve Burdett is a writer based in London, England—a city where some of the people in these pages rocked, ruled, bickered, and backstabbed. He is the author of several books, and he hopes that this, written around the time of the birth of his first child, might provide a little laughter to lighten history for children everywhere.

 hinkler

Published by Hinkler Books Pty Ltd
45–55 Fairchild Street
Heatherton Victoria 3202 Australia
www.hinkler.com

© Hinkler Books Pty Ltd 2017

Author: Steve Burdett
Illustrator: Glen Singleton
Front-cover illustrator: Rob Kiely
Cover design: Hinkler Design Studio
Internal design: Trudi Webb
Prepress: Graphic Print Group

ISBN: 978 1 4889 0867 5

Printed and bound in China

Contents

Introduction

In the Beginnng

I f you're the type of person who falls asleep at the back of the class during history lessons, you'll never have that problem again!

Saying you think history is boring is a bit like saying you think fighter planes, space travel, knights on horseback, mighty queens, samurai warriors, nutty professors, witches, and pirates are boring. The history of the world is packed full of the coolest and most hilarious things you can imagine!

This book will take you way back in time to see some of the spectacular things that people did back then, like building the pyramids, exploring the world and discovering places like America and Australia in rickety old ships, putting people on trial for being witches, and giving out the worst kind of medicine you can imagine!

You'll visit the Wild West and its most famous cowboys, meet the notorious Genghis Khan, and encounter the great figures of Europe (who really liked fighting each other all the time). You'll learn about the unsinkable ship that sank and the brilliant woman who carried radioactive test tubes in her pocket. We'll show you why adults tell you that eating carrots will help you see in the dark and we'll reveal what people used to wipe their bottoms with before they invented toilet paper.

Then we're going to bring things right up to the 21st century, with the invention of things like the motor car, the airplane, rocket ships, and the home computer. There'd be no computer tablets or smartphones without them!

Of course, it wouldn't be history if we didn't include some dire diseases, greedy queens, big-headed bullies, and the baddest bad guys. These people are seriously worse than anything you have seen in a movie—so be warned! And, as you'll see, there are plenty of great heroes of history to offer hope and give stories a happy ending.

You see, history is where the greatest stories ever told (as well as the greatest storytellers) come from. Movies and TV shows get lots of inspiration from history, and just about every school play today has something to thank the brilliant William Shakespeare for.

So, our history is full of heroes and villains, the greedy and the good, and geniuses and schemers. It's this combination that makes the history of our world such an awesome, amazing, and often hilarious story—so strap yourself in. It's going to be a really cool ride!

A Long, Long Time Ago ...

The Ancient Egyptians, Greeks, and Romans

1 Ancient Egypt's Game of Thrones

Queen Nefertiti, who ruled from around 1353 to 1336 BC, was one of the most famous women in Ancient Egypt. Her name means "the beautiful one has come!" She's a bit of a celebrity even now, thanks to the 1913 discovery of a bust of her that backed up those ancient claims about her beauty.

Nefertiti was the wife of the pharaoh Akhenaten. They had six daughters together, but as Akhenaten wanted a son he married several other women as well. This included marrying his own sister (huh?!), with whom he had a son called Tutankhamun. Tutankhamun later married his own half-sister (Nefertiti's

daughter!). Just imagine how awkward family reunions must have been …

Cleopatra VII was the last queen of Egypt and took to the throne in 51 BC when she was only seventeen years old. She married two of her brothers, and she is believed to have killed the second one to put her son on the throne! The higher the status of a person in Egyptian society, the more makeup they wore—and Cleopatra wore a lot. Interestingly, both women and men wore makeup in Egyptian times. Cleopatra was famed for her beauty, she was super smart, and she spoke several languages. She had a great romance and political alliance with the Roman general Marc Antony. It ended sadly

though: in 30 BC, they both took their own lives after losing a battle to decide the new Roman emperor, Marc Antony being defeated by a Roman called Augustus (63 BC—14 AD).

Did you know?

Female pharaoh Hatshepsut wore men's clothes and a false beard because she believed that this would bring her closer to the Egyptian gods! The longest reigning female pharaoh, she ruled for 20 years in the 15th century BC and was one of Egypt's most successful rulers.

Tomb Raiders

Anyone who has played the Tomb Raider video game or has seen the films will have been impressed by the archaeological exploits of Lara Croft. But did you know she wasn't the original tomb raider?

The Ancient Egyptians believed that after death, their souls lived on and so they needed a body to travel to the afterlife. Corpses were preserved in embalming fluids, wrapped up in bandages, and turned into mummies. The wealthiest Egyptians were buried with all their gold, jewels, and anything else that they'd need in the afterlife. The pharaohs were laid to rest in the grandest tombs of all: the pyramids.

With so much treasure inside these tombs, robbers could hardly resist breaking into them. As punishment, however, anyone caught robbing a tomb was killed in a way that guaranteed they wouldn't get into the afterlife, which was bad news indeed for an Egyptian. The tombs had secret doors and traps set up inside to prevent them being pillaged, and curses were sworn upon those who would steal from them.

In 1922, an archaeological team opened the tomb of
Tutankhamun, who had been buried around 1323 BC.
Members of the team began to die shortly afterwards from
different causes: a mysterious illness, blood poisoning, an
infected mosquito bite, and a fever. One was assassinated and
another was even shot by his wife. Were they unrelated freak
incidents, or was this the famous curse of the pharaohs?

Did you know?

Ancient Egyptians believed that magic
could cure illness, poison their
enemies, protect the king, and charm
scorpions. They even had magic wands
made from ivory. Eat your heart out, Harry Potter!

3 Greek Gods and Myths

The Ancient Greeks loved a good myth, and we still read about their ancient stories today. One of the most famous is the story of the Trojan Horse.

According to legend, the Greeks were fighting the Trojans, who were from Troy, which was an ancient city in present-day Turkey. The Greeks laid siege to Troy for ten years, and by then were no doubt bored by this continual attack on the city. So, they built a huge wooden horse, hid some soldiers in it, and made it look like they'd all sailed away. Thinking it was a tribute to the goddess of war, Athena, the Trojans (let's face it, hardly the brightest bunch) brought the Trojan horse into their city. In the dead of night, the Greek soldiers got out of the horse and opened the city gates, letting their pals in to conquer the city. D'oh!

The Greeks also loved their gods. Daddy of all the gods was Zeus, the god of thunder and ruler of Mount Olympus: the home of the gods. The gods watched over the lives of the mortals down on Earth. The Greeks lived in fear of making the gods angry and with good reason: people believed they could send down thunderbolts, sink ships, start earthquakes, and generally make life really, really unpleasant.

Zeus will never know if I steal one of his two stuffed olives.

Did you know?

In the original Olympic Games, which began all the way back in 776 BC, all the athletes competed naked! Original events included chariot racing and wrestling, and all the events were held in honor of Zeus.

Running the marathon naked is so wrong ...without sandals, my feet are killing me!

4 Alexander the Great

One of the most powerful head honchos in the ancient world was undoubtedly Alexander the Great, a man who never lost a battle. But Alexander wasn't just a tough guy. He loved music and reading, and he was taught by the scientist and philosopher Aristotle, one of the great Greek geeks.

With both brawn and brains on his side, Alexander became king when his dad was assassinated in 336 BC. He then started doing some conquering—lots of it. He conquered Egypt, where he founded the city of Alexandria, which, less than modestly, he named after himself. He expanded and ruled over an empire that stretched from Greece all the way to India.

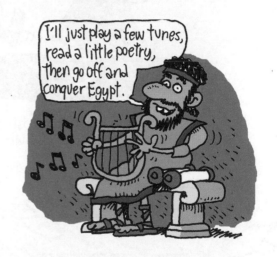

Alexander could get a bit big-headed, maybe because he read too much about the gods and legendary heroes like Achilles, or maybe because he listened to his ambitious mother Olympias. He claimed that he was the son of the Greek god Zeus and believed that he was invincible in battle. (To be fair, he never was beaten!) He took big risks, which his soldiers didn't always like, and he also started to adopt the clothes and mannerisms of the Persian Empire, which his countrymen

really didn't like. But if anyone plotted against Alexander, he'd just have them executed. I guess that's one way to stop people grumbling …

OK …OK…OK! I only meant that I preferred them in blue!

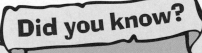

Alexander shows off his new Persian shoes and deals with anyone who doesn't appreciate them.

Did you know?

No army or man could beat Alexander the Great, but a legion of germs was too much for him. He died of a fever in 323 BC.

5 The Geeky Greeks

The Ancient Greeks had some super-smart people among them. Their big-brained philosophers, scientists, engineers, astronomers, and mathematicians had a huge influence on the world.

Pythagoras, who is best known today for his theorem on right-angled triangles, was a mathematician and philosopher whose name still earns a groan from students in math class over 2,500 years after he died.

Archimedes was an amazing inventor. The King of Syracuse asked Archimedes to work out if his crown was made from pure gold or if he had been cheated by its maker. The idea of how to work this out came to Archimedes one day when he stepped in the bath. "Eureka!" he cried (meaning, "I've got it!"), and he ran naked through the streets in excitement. He had worked out that the displacement of the water was the same as the mass of the object (or, in his case, person) displacing it. The geeky Greeks knew the mass of gold, so they could see how much water was displaced by the crown and figure out

whether it was made from real gold. Proof that bath time isn't always wasted time!

Did you know?

Among Archimedes' many inventions were the catapult, which was used to defend his homeland from the invading Romans, and his coolest invention (or hottest, really): a heat ray made from mirrors that set fire to enemy ships.

6 Julius Caesar

Julius Caesar was one of the great dictators of history. As a general in the army he conquered a town called Gaul, which was in present-day France and Western Europe. Then in 49 BC he went back to Italy and started an almighty civil war, after which he became the supreme leader of the Romans. If there was one thing the Romans did an awful lot of, it was fighting.

Caesar was a popular guy. In between destroying his enemies, he dated the Egyptian queen Cleopatra, and he tried to sort out Roman society by doing things like reducing Rome's huge debts. What thanks did he get for this? In 44 BC, the senators thought Caesar was getting a little too big for his sandals and he was famously assassinated by Brutus (a Roman politician) and other senators on the festival of the Ides of March (March 15th).

Did you know?

Caesar's assassins did not judge the public's feelings on Caesar correctly and his assassination caused a civil war to break out. Instead of becoming a Republic as the senators had hoped, Caesar's great-nephew Augustus eventually became emperor of Rome. (Remember, he was the guy who beat Marc Antony—Cleopatra's love!)

7 Pompeii

Pompeii was a bustling Roman town in the south of Italy that showed off some of the Romans' best engineering feats and customs, like an amphitheater, where Romans watched chariot races and gladiators fighting, and a gymnasium, where people bathed and trained. Even in Roman times there was no escape from gym class!

But Pompeii was no match for the nearby Mount Vesuvius, which erupted in 79 AD. The volcano spewed out gas

I'm not really worried about some old volcano exploding Tiberius. A chariot has just lost a wheel on the last lap of this race!

and ash that was so hot and so fast that it killed anyone in its way whether they were eating dinner or sitting on the toilet. Mostly, they were running for their lives. The town was buried in layers of ash and forgotten for hundreds of years.

In the 18th century, Pompeii was finally excavated, and today it's one of the best-preserved archaeological sites in the world. Visitors can walk on streets that haven't changed for over 1,600 years to see what life was like then. The ash preserved the final postures of over a thousand people, and today visitors can see cast outlines of their bodies.

Do you mind?

Did you know?

Historical artifacts weren't the only things preserved in the volcano's ash: graffiti was too! Things like "Marcus loves Spendusa" and "Aufidius was here" were found scrawled in Latin on the walls of buildings, proving that some things, like graffiti, never change!

Augustus leaving Pompeii really quickly!

8 Gladiators

Today we watch sports or concerts in stadiums, but back in Roman times, stadiums were where people enjoyed watching the bloody spectacle of combat!

A gladiator's job was to entertain crowds by fighting with other gladiators. They were usually—but not always—slaves. Men occasionally volunteered, either for money or to prove themselves. They must have been mad! Some gladiators fought with a sword and shield while others had nothing but a net and a trident (a three-pronged spear), which seems a little unfair! The amphitheaters where the contests took place were brutal places. The crowd would go wild, desperate to see a gladiator beaten or, if the gladiator had fought well and entertained the crowd, cheering for them to be spared. Spectators held out their thumbs to determine if the losing gladiator was to be spared

or not, although today it's unclear which gesture meant what! At the Colosseum in Rome, the emperor made the ultimate call, although it was best for him not to go against the crowd's wishes, as it could cause riots. People also watched men fight bears and lions, and even saw some poor folk get thrown to the lions!

Gladiators won wreaths for their victories, and the better ones became heroes to the people, just like the sporting heroes we celebrate today in our arenas.

Did you know?

The most famous gladiator of all was Spartacus, who led a great uprising of slaves against the Romans. He freed so many slaves he soon had an army of his own. There was even a blockbuster film made about him in 1960.

9 Hadrian's Wall

Emperor Hadrian started work on a wall in the north of England in 122 AD, supposedly to separate the Romans from the "barbarians" in the north, who were famously fierce in battle. The Romans never managed to conquer these people, who were a group of tribes called the Picts that lived in present-day eastern and northern Scotland. You can see how a wall to keep out a noisy and bothersome neighbor might appeal.

The wall covered the whole width of the country, some 73 miles (over 117 km) long. Small garrisons of troops were stationed along the wall, as well as bigger forts that housed as many as a thousand troops. These soldiers came from all over the Roman Empire, so you'd find soldiers from places as diverse as Spain,

Belgium, and northern Africa. They all shared the communal toilets, which didn't have cubicles but were just long wooden benches with holes in them. You could look at and chat to your friends while you did your business. Sound like fun? Well, maybe not once you learn that there was no toilet paper: the soldiers shared a sponge on a stick to wipe themselves!

Did you know?

By 410 AD, the Romans struggled to maintain their empire, so they left Britain to take care of matters closer to home. A lot of the Hadrian Wall still stands to this day. An original wooden toilet seat was even discovered there in 2014!

Vicious Invaders

The Medieval Period

10 Viking Raiders

Disappointingly, the Vikings never actually had horns on their helmets, but the stories of their brutal raids are certainly true.

Hailing from Scandinavia—the region comprised of Norway, Denmark and Sweden—the Vikings set sail in longships to raid countries like Britain and France. They had no problem at all with attacking monasteries, stealing from them, and sometimes burning them to the ground. They really, really liked doing this.

The Vikings fought with swords and axes, and they had champion warriors known as "berserkers." As their name suggests, these guys literally went berserk. They wouldn't bother with tiny details like armor: instead they wore bear

or wolf skins, howled at the moon, and generally worked themselves up into a furious, trance-like frenzy. This caused them to perform seemingly superhuman acts of strength and speed, and to indiscriminately attack all those around them!

But the Vikings weren't just fearsome warriors and destroyers. They were first-rate sea dogs and explorers, voyaging to far-off places like North Africa and North America. They were tradesmen too, and traveled as far as Constantinople in Turkey to trade goods—and slaves.

Did you know?

Can anyone else smell smoke?

The Vikings loved boats so much that when an important person died, their bodies were put in a burial ship along with their possessions. The ship was either buried or sent out to sea in flames.

11 Norse Mythology

If you thought Thor and Loki were just a couple of cool characters from the Avengers, then you'd better read on …

According to Norse mythology, Odin was ruler of the gods and the god of magic, poetry, and war. He rode an eight-legged horse, which isn't even the weirdest animal in the myths! His eldest son was Thor, the god of thunder, whose weapon of choice was an almighty hammer. He liked his hammer so much, he gave it a name—Mjolnir, which doesn't exactly slip off the tongue today.

What is it about Thor's family? They've always got to have the biggest hammer and the horse with the most legs.

Try galloping with eight legs and not getting them tangled!

The Norse believed that a lightning flash was Thor throwing his hammer, and a thunderstorm was Thor riding his chariot—pulled by goats—in the sky. He had a short temper and loved nothing more than thumping giants—the enemies of the gods—with Mjolnir.

Loki was a shape-shifting god who could become a fish, a bird, or an old lady. He was, frankly, a bit of a troublemaker. Though not related to Thor by blood, he was every inch the annoying younger brother, playing pranks whenever he could for his own amusement. When his jokes wore thin, the other gods tied him to a rock where a serpent dripped poison on him. The Vikings believed that earthquakes were caused by Loki struggling to get away from the serpent.

Did you know?

Thor's chariot-pulling goats were a handy snack for him: as long as their bones remained intact, he could eat them and they were simply reborn!

12 Norman Conquest

One date etched on every British schoolkid's memory is 1066: the year of the Battle of Hastings.

When the Anglo-Saxon king Edward the Confessor died, it sparked a three-way no-holds-barred battle over who would rule England. In the Anglo-Saxon corner was Harold II, who had taken the crown. In the Viking corner was Harald Hardrada, king of Norway, who had help from Harold II's own brother! Finally, in the Norman corner was William, Duke of Normandy in northern France.

The Vikings landed first, and Harold headed north to Yorkshire and fought them in a bloody battle, killing the Viking king and his brother in the process. He probably thought he'd earned a rest after that, but wait … who's that in the south? It's the Normans landing from France!

A dog-tired Harold marched south to fight William of Normandy, but this time Harold's army was no match for the Normans. William's army had many archers and knights on horseback, while Harold's army only had foot soldiers. The Norman army pretended to run away, so the Anglo-Saxons chased after them, but Harold soon saw the error of his ways … just before he saw the arrow that hit him in the eye, killing him—yikes!

Did you know?

William the Conqueror loved feasting almost as much as he loved fighting. He became so fat that he couldn't get on his horse. His idea for a diet? To stop eating food and just drink alcohol. As you can guess, it was not a success!

This is not going to happen is it, William?

Knights in Shining Armor

The knights were the coolest warriors in medieval times. With their armor, coats of arms, swords, and lances, they certainly looked the part. They lived by the Code of Chivalry, which meant that they would defend the Church and always behave honorably and bravely … or so it appeared. In fact, knights were a bit selective about when they used the code. For instance, they didn't always think chivalry applied to peasants.

Knights started their training young, learning to fight from about the age of twelve or thirteen. And you thought school could be tough! Then they could become squires, acting as a knight's assistant by carrying his equipment and even heading on to the battlefield with him. At twenty-one, they could become knights themselves.

Did you know?

On the battlefield, you could identify each knight by their coats of arms and the plumes in their helmets, a bit like sports stars do today with their uniforms and player numbers!

14 The Crusades

In medieval times, the Muslim world stretched from Spain to India. Christians in Jerusalem were increasingly persecuted by the city's Islamic rulers. This didn't sit well with Pope Urban II. In 1095, he called for the knights of Europe to seize control of Jerusalem in the name of Christianity, in what would become known as the First Crusade.

The promise of seeing the world, glory in battle, and even forgiveness for past sins were all strong motivations for knights to join the Crusade. Unfortunately, the armies were far from beacons of holy action and they couldn't resist getting stuck into such serious pillaging and slaying that it would have made even the Vikings blush. When they finally got to the holy city of Jerusalem, they killed the city's Muslim and Jewish citizens.

What were they thinking with this get-up for fighting in the heat? What I need is a cold drink and a pair of shorts.

Over the next 200 years, more Crusades were launched, with plenty more opportunities to cause mayhem in the name of religion. Although the Christians didn't fare as well in these later Crusades, they did expose themselves to a lot of sophisticated knowledge and learnt about the ways of life in the Muslim world. This included their numbering system (which definitely beat using Roman numerals!), medical advances, and the trade of goods such as spices, silk, and sugar.

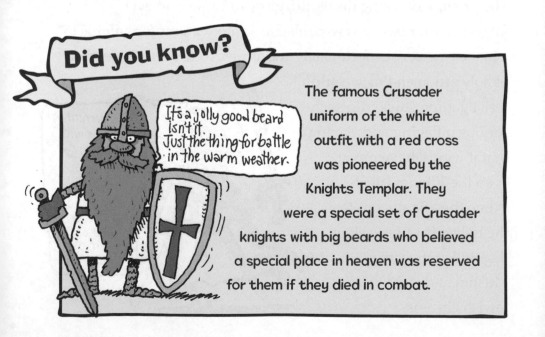

Did you know?

The famous Crusader uniform of the white outfit with a red cross was pioneered by the Knights Templar. They were a special set of Crusader knights with big beards who believed a special place in heaven was reserved for them if they died in combat.

15 The Black Death

The most devastating invasion in history wasn't man-made: it was disease. A terrible plague called the Black Death swept across the world around 1346—1353. The plague wiped out around a third of Europe's population and killed so many millions of people that it took centuries for the world's population to return to pre-plague levels. The disease was believed to have started in China. It was carried by fleas that lived on the rats that traveled along trade routes with transported goods. People lived in filthy conditions, with no drains or flush toilets, meaning rats always found a comfortable home to spread the disease from town to town.

The plague caused great pus-oozing boils to swell up on the skin. Next would come fever, vomiting blood, and, after just a matter of days, death. You really didn't want to catch this bug!

Medical knowledge wasn't exactly very helpful. Medical people at the time didn't have a clue what was causing the disease: if no other explanation was forthcoming, they just assumed it was a punishment from God for their sins. Others decided it was the fault of lepers or beggars, so the treatment should be attacking these poor people. The little medical treatment that was on offer included patients whipping themselves, tying a live chicken to themselves, or (ew!) drinking their own urine!

Did you know?

When laying siege to the Italian city of Kaffa in 1347, some soldiers in the Mongol army became infected by the Black Death. When these soldiers had passed away, the Mongols threw the corpses into the city to infect their enemy. Now that's fighting dirty!

16 Medieval Medicine

Getting sick during medieval times could quite literally be a real pain. It's very likely that your body would not only consider an infection to be a vicious invader but also think about the doctor who was meant to be treating it in the same way!

People still believed in the Ancient Greek idea that the body contained four "humors"—blood, black bile, phlegm, and yellow bile—and that curing disease meant balancing out these bodily fluids. This often meant draining some blood, so doctors would make a cut and leave it to bleed or use leeches to suck a patient's blood. A doctor might give a patient something to make them throw up or even drill holes into their skull (called "trepanning"). It sounds more like torture (which happened a lot of during this time) than medicine!

We shouldn't be too hard on medieval doctors: many of these methods were still being used well into the 18th century, and leeches are still used today to drain blood to help burn victims

with skin grafts and even in re-attaching body parts, like fingers. And it wasn't all bad. With many vicious invaders fighting wars, it meant there were plenty of opportunities to practice and improve surgical techniques. It was discovered that using herbs and alcohol as an anesthetic helped, though unfortunately they still hadn't figured out that dirty conditions will cause infections. D'oh!

Did you know?

Barbers also worked as surgeons and dentists! The traditional red-and-white colors on a barber's pole came from red blood and the white napkins that barber-surgeons used. Don't ask a barber to perform surgery on you today—that's what hospitals are for!

Ye Olde
BARBER
SHOP
Haircuts
Minor Surgery
Troublesome
Teeth Pulled

Deadly Dynasties

The Chinese, Mongol, and Russian Empires

17 The Song Dynasty

The 11th and 12th centuries were a great time for China. Under the Song dynasty (a family that ruled for several generations), China became one of the most advanced civilizations in the world. During this period, China developed the first official permanent navy and sailed to Korea, Japan, India, and Sri Lanka. The Chinese pioneered the use of the compass for navigation, banknotes, and moveable type printing, which they used to educate their people.

The Chinese also came to grips with gunpowder, and not just for fireworks. They made bombs from gunpowder and scrap metal and launched them from catapults. They also made early forms of rockets, flamethrowers (which they called "fire lances"), and landmines. These weapons helped keep the Chinese empire safe from their enemies for centuries.

With smoking-hot inventions like these, someone was bound to want to steal them! The Song regime allied with the Mongols to defeat a rival dynasty called the Jin, but they didn't think it through properly. The Mongols decided to conquer the Song armies too, which they did by using some of the Song dynasty's own weapons against them!

Did you know?

During the Song dynasty, the practice of tightly binding the feet of young girls to stop their feet growing became popular. Little feet were considered a sign of beauty. These poor girls may have had little feet, but they also experienced great pain for fashion!

18 Genghis Khan

Genghis Khan, who came to power in 1206, was the founder of the great Mongol Empire. This was the largest land empire in history, covering much of China and Asia. But Genghis Khan is also famous for being plain mean!

Genghis wanted to establish trade links with the Khwarazmian dynasty of western Asia. They weren't so keen and sent Genghis's envoy back … minus their heads! The Khwarazmian dynasty, however, were about to learn that you don't mess with Genghis Khan and his army of excellent horsemen.

The Mongols went on the offensive and attacked a Khwarazmian city, killing absolutely everyone—including the cats and dogs! They made pyramids out of heads, which wouldn't have impressed the Egyptians. The Mongols had Chinese weapons such as gunpowder and catapults, and used them to wipe the entire

Khwarazmian empire off the map. That's one way to show you're not pleased!

Despite this, Genghis had a pretty liberal attitude towards religion. His empire included Christians, Buddhists, Muslims, and people of many other belief systems, which is pretty cool when you think about the brutal and less-tolerant Crusades that were happening at the time.

Did you know?

Genghis Khan created one of the world's first international postal services. The Mongols had post offices all over the empire and delivered mail by horseback.

19 Marco Polo

Marco Polo was an explorer and merchant from Venice. In 1271, he set off on a journey with his father and uncle, and didn't come home for twenty-four years!

Marco was one of the first Westerners to visit China. He visited during the Juan dynasty, when China was ruled by the emperor Kublai Khan. Kublai was a Mongol leader and was the grandson of Genghis Khan.

Kublai Khan took a liking to Marco and welcomed him into his palace. Marco worked for him for seventeen years and traveled all over China, taking part in adventures and encountering animals he'd never seen before, like elephants and crocodiles.

When it was time to return home, Marco Polo came back a wealthy man, but his native city of Venice was fighting with Genoa. He led his ship into battle, was captured by the Genoans, and was thrown in prison. Marco told his story to his cellmate, an Italian romance writer, who wrote it down, but he might have embellished things just a teeny bit! The book was

called *The Travels of Marco Polo* and it was a big hit, but not with everyone. Some thought Marco was a liar and had made it all up, which some people still think today!

Did you know?

On his travels, Marco Polo thought he'd discovered a unicorn ... but it turned out to be a rhinoceros. D'oh!

20 The Samurai

Japanese samurai were traditionally warriors who served wealthy masters. At the end of the 12th century, however, they came to prominence with the rise of the first shogun—a

military ruler who held the real power in contrast to the emperor, who was more of a figurehead.

The samurai were famous for their sword, known as a katana, but it wasn't the only weapon they used. They used longbows and spears and, when they encountered gunpowder, they were more than happy to use that too!

Kublai Khan's Mongols twice sailed to Japan to invade, in 1274 and 1281. Although the samurai were outnumbered, thunderstorms and a typhoon sent the Mongols back both times. The samurai believed that the kamikaze—"divine wind"—had sent their enemy away.

Samurai lived by a strict code, and if a samurai was disgraced, he had an opportunity to regain his honor … by ritually stabbing himself! This didn't give much room for second chances.

Did you know?

Raijin was the Japanese god of thunder, lightning, and storms, and in ancient times people believed that he hammered his drums to make thunder. Some parents in Japan still tell their children to hide their belly buttons during a thunderstorm, as Raijin was known to try and eat navels!

21 The Great Wall and the Forbidden City

The Great Wall of China is 5,500 miles (8,850 km) long, which makes it the biggest man-made structure in the world. It was started by the Qin dynasty back in 220 BC, but most of the wall we see today was built under the Ming dynasty. It was built to protect China from the Mongols, who had been kicked out by the Chinese in 1368 AD.

During this time, the Chinese sailed to the Middle East and Africa to trade. Among many things, the Chinese made pretty Ming vases, some of which are worth a fortune today. They also built the Forbidden City in Beijing, which was home to the emperor and the biggest palace complex in the world.

I'll be glad to get home to the open spaces of Mongolia. That place is too crowded anyway!

Ordinary people couldn't just turn up to the Forbidden City without an invitation, as the punishment was death. In fact, only the emperor was really welcome in the Forbidden City, along with his many girlfriends, who all lived there together. Emperor Yongle was the first to live there, and he wasn't above being brutal. He stole the throne from his nephew, killed thousands of his enemies, and when he died in 1424, some of his girlfriends were forced to die too, proving he could be just as tyrannical from the afterlife.

Oh! How disappointing! I guess I'll have to go count the bricks in the Great Wall instead.

FORBIDDEN CITY CLOSED TODAY

Did you know?

Despite what some people claim, the Great Wall of China cannot be seen from space with the naked eye. Chinese textbooks corrected this misconception after the first Chinese man in space, Yang Liwei, confirmed he couldn't see it in 2004.

A shame you can't see the Great Wall from up here in space. I wonder if Mum can see me waving.

22 Ivan the Terrible

Ivan Vasilyevich (commonly known as Ivan the Terrible) became the first Tsar (ruler) of all Russia in 1547. He was a smart man who forged links with Europe and introduced the printing press to his country. Oh, and he was also a mad tyrant!

He didn't get off to the best start in life. He became Grand Prince of Russia after his dad died when he was only three years old, so his mother had to hold the throne for him until he was old enough to rule. Unfortunately, she was poisoned when he was only eight.

Ivan had a vicious temper. At the age of 13, he had a rival killed. He had it in for the old nobility, who he thought were plotting against him, and he destroyed the town

Oh he's cranky this one! I think I'll call him Ivan.... Ivan the Terrible.

of Novgorod on a paranoid hunch. In the middle of an argument with his eldest son and heir, he struck him with a staff—and accidentally killed him!

Ivan had seven wives during his life, outdoing even Henry VIII of England, who only had six. For such a violent man, it's incredible that Ivan died while he was engaging in a much more sedate form of combat than he would find on the battlefield: he was playing chess!

I had a terrible holiday in Novgorod once.

Destroy the place!

Did you know?

Ivan the Terrible proposed to Queen Elizabeth I of England, but she turned him down. This made him mad and he wrote a very rude letter to her to express his disappointment!

There's a letter here from an Ivan the Terrible asking for your hand in marriage my Queen.

Ivan the terrible? Oh, he sounds like a really nice man!

Cities of Gold

The Aztecs, Incas, and the New World

23 Have a Heart, Aztecs!

The Aztecs dominated much of Mexico between the 14th and 16th centuries. The center of their civilization was a city called Tenochtitlan (where Mexico City is today). According to legend, Tenochtitlan was built on a site that had been chosen by the Aztec god Huitzilopochtli, the god of … war, sun and human sacrifice!

My dearest daughter. Just pop on over and marry the next door neighbor to keep the peace. He's tall, dark handsome and bloodthirsty.

Just my sort of guy Dad.!

The Aztecs loved a good human sacrifice, and it was

always better to sacrifice their neighbors than to have to use their own people; though, at a pinch, they would do this too. The preferred method was for a temple priest to remove the unfortunate victim's heart—while it was still beating!

They didn't do this for fun. The Aztecs believed that human sacrifice would repay the debt they owed to the gods for creating humans and the world, and that without paying these sacrifices, the sun—the source of all light— would go out.

The Aztecs fought endless wars with their neighbors and built an impressive empire. Their most fearsome soldiers were the Eagle and Jaguar warriors, who wore terrifying battle outfits (feathers for the Eagle warriors and jaguar pelts for the Jaguars) and whose main goal was to capture, not kill, the enemy. No prizes for guessing what they did with their prisoners.

Did you know?

Tenochtitlan was built on an island in a lake, and it was a prosperous city with a canal system and floating gardens on the water.

24 Incas: The People in the Clouds

The Incas lived on and around the Andes mountains in Peru. Their leader Pachacuti was the South American equivalent of Alexander the Great: he loved conquering, and he did lots of it. He was the Sapa Inca from 1438–71, which meant he was considered the son of the sun—a big deal to his sun-worshipping people. The Incas believed they had to keep the gods of the mountains happy, which they did through human sacrifice.

Pachacuti transformed his small kingdom into the great Inca Empire, which covered a vast area of western South America and was home to as many as ten million people. He built a stunning summer home in the sky called Machu Picchu, complete with rope bridges like something out of an adventure movie. Some of them are still in use today!

When the Incas conquered rival tribes, they would take the children of the tribal leaders and send them off to boarding school in the capital city, Cusco. The children would have to learn the language and discover how to be good Inca citizens and to not start any kind of rebellion!

Did you know?

Inca noblemen wore discs within holes in their ears that were big enough to significantly stretch their earlobes. The Spanish nicknamed them Orejones, which means big ears!

25 Sun Worshippers

Both the Incas and the Aztecs loved gold. It was, as it is today, a symbol of wealth and power. They also believed that gold was the sweat of the sun and silver was the tears of the moon. The Incas even buried their dead with their gold and silver.

Also, the Incas and Aztecs both worshipped the sun. The Aztecs believed that this world was that of the fifth sun. Four had already been created and destroyed … and one day this world would be too! Typically, the Aztecs' sun god, Huitzilopochtli, was also their god of war.

Their agriculture systems were sophisticated and their busy markets saw things like food, animal skins, gold, and bird feathers being traded. They ate a lot of things that we now do today. If your parents imagine themselves to be fashionable food lovers, they might like to eat a grain called quinoa. (They might be pronouncing it wrong, too: it's keen-wa!) But the Incas and the Aztecs were eating this hundreds of years ago. They were also getting stuck into potatoes, tomatoes, avocados, beans, and chili peppers. If none of that has you salivating at the thought of eating it, just wait, because they also had chocolate!

Did you know?

The Aztecs played a ball game where they scored points through hoops, a bit like basketball. Only their hips, elbows, and knees (not their hands or feet) could be used.

The stakes were high, as the losing team was sacrificed!

26 Clueless Chris

Christopher Columbus was an Italian sailor and explorer in the 15th and 16th centuries. He was credited with discovering the Americas, which came as news to the millions of people already living there, not to mention the Vikings who'd sailed there 500 years earlier.

In 1492, Columbus set sail on a voyage financed by Spain, going west to discover a new route to the Far East. When the call of "Land ho!" went out, Columbus was thrilled to have discovered a new part of Asia to colonize. But Chris was pretty clueless: in fact, he had landed in the Caribbean. Oops!

Columbus made three more voyages to what became known as the New World (the name given to the Americas). He explored Central and South America, which Christopher thought was still Asia, and he brought back gold and tobacco.

Due to his exploits, he was considered a hero in Spain, but his gift to the New World? As governor, he killed and enslaved many of the locals. When reports of his tyranny finally reached the king and queen of Spain, he was arrested when he returned home. But if the New World inhabitants thought Columbus was bad, they sadly hadn't seen anything yet.

Did you know?

Despite Columbus "discovering" the New World, the Americas were named after Italian explorer, navigator, and cartographer Amerigo Vespucci, who was the first to point out that the Americas were different continents to Asia.

27 Cortés's Gold

Hernando Cortés was a conquistador—a Spanish soldier and explorer. He was to be the commander of an expedition to Mexico: a place Cortés was more interested in for its Aztec gold than its cultural value. When his mission was cancelled, Cortés disobeyed his orders and went anyway.

When he got to Mexico, Cortés traveled to the capital of the Aztecs. On the way, he made friends with lots of the Aztecs' neighbors, who understandably might have held a grudge with the Aztecs over all the warring and sacrifices the Aztecs had practiced on their populations.

The Aztec leader Montezuma II thought Cortés might be a kind of white god. He greeted Cortés with gold and other gifts. In return, Cortés took him hostage. That's gratitude for you! With the help of the local tribes, Cortés conquered the Aztecs, though he could thank one vicious invader for the victory: disease, especially smallpox. The Aztecs had no immunity to it, so it

The Aztecs, Incas, and the New World

killed many of them and gravely weakened their army. The Aztecs that survived smallpox as well as the Spanish swords were forced to convert to Christianity, and many were made slaves.

Did you know?

Cortés was, if nothing else, a great motivator. To stop his men fleeing from battle with the imposing Aztecs, he sank his own fleet of ships!

28 The End of the Incas

In the name of bringing Christianity to the "heathens" and to gain as much land and gold as possible, the Spanish Empire spread to South America from Mexico, where they came into conflict with the Incas.

This time, greedy conquistador Hernando Pizarro led the way. In 1532, he met with the Inca leader Atahualpa and his people, and promptly attacked them! The Incas were stunned by the sight of the guns and horses: they'd never seen anything like them before and were soon overwhelmed. Atahualpa was kidnapped and held for a heavy ransom.

The Incas paid the ransom, but the Spanish didn't let him go. Instead, they forced him to convert to Christianity ... but then they killed him anyway! With the leader out the way, plus the unwelcome gift of smallpox from the Spanish, the Incas were easily conquered. The Spanish were dazzled by the sight of the beautiful artifacts made from Inca gold and loaded their ships to take it home with them.

> Captain. We've overloaded the ship with our hoard of gold and treasure!

> Oh no! Quick – Save the ship! Throw the food overboard.

> I'm staying here in the Amazon forever with all of this Inca treasure!

> What are we going to spend it on though?

Did you know?

Paititi is a mythical Inca city of gold somewhere deep in the Amazon jungle, which, according to legend, is home to untold riches. Some of the archeologists and adventurers that have gone in search of it have never returned ...

Rocking the Renaissance

Kings, Queens, Culture, Science, and Suspicion

29 The Spanish Inquisition

Queen Isabella and King Ferdinand ruled over Spain, and were enlightened enough to sponsor Christopher Columbus's explorations around the world. But they also were in charge during the Spanish Inquisition, which the Spanish don't remember as fondly.

Isabella and Ferdinand wanted to make Spain a united Catholic country, and so they forced their Muslim and Jewish inhabitants to convert. The Inquisition was established in 1478 and was basically a test to make sure these converted people were being good Catholics. While you might think of a test today as being torture, this test really did involve torture.

were being good Catholics. While you might think of a test today as being torture, this test really did involve torture.

In order to get a confession, the inquisitors used torture devices such as the rack, where the accused would have their wrists and ankles chained to rollers and the rollers were turned, stretching their body and breaking their bones. Then there was the strappado, where the victim would have their arms tied behind their back and they'd be hung from the ceiling by them, which was very painful.

There were also less elaborate measures such as thumbscrews, which slowly crushed fingers, or red-hot pincers. Even if you survived all this but were found guilty, you'd then be burnt alive at the stake!

Did you know?

Despite her part in the Inquisition, Queen Isabella was a patron of the arts and learned Latin at the age of 35. She was also the first woman ever to appear on a coin in the US, in 1893.

30 Da Vinci and the *Mona Lisa*

The *Mona Lisa* is arguably the most famous painting in the world. A lot of people debate whether she is smiling or not. Its Italian painter Leonardo da Vinci possessed a brain big enough to match the greatest Greek geeks; he was actually a bit of a fan of them and of their scientific approach to knowledge.

Leonardo was around during a period known as the Renaissance (meaning rebirth), which lasted from the 14th to the 17th centuries.

During this time, great advances in science and culture happened, and Leonardo, who lived from 1452 to 1519, was the boy in class who could do it all: he was an ace at art, perfect at painting, and incredible at inventing! The expression "Renaissance man" was invented for geniuses who were good at many different things, like Leonardo!

Leonardo produced concept designs for a helicopter and a parachute long before they were invented. His drawing *Vitruvian Man* and his painting *The Last Supper* are almost as famous as the *Mona Lisa*. Fellow Renaissance man Michelangelo was pretty handy too, sculpting a statue of the biblical giant-slayer David in the nude and painting the ceiling of the Sistine Chapel: a decorating job that took four years! Along with sculptor Donatello and painter and architect Raphael, these guys were so cool that the Teenage Mutant Ninja Turtles were named after them!

Did you know?

Over the years, the *Mona Lisa* has had acid, a rock, paint, and a teacup thrown at her in the Louvre gallery in Paris, and in 1911 she was stolen by someone who kept her in his apartment for two years.

Today, more than six million visitors a year come to look at the painting and take selfies, but now through bulletproof glass!

31 Horrid Henry VIII

Henry VIII was a good-looking English prince in the 16th century who loved sport and learning. He desperately wanted to be known as a Renaissance king ... but became better known for his bulging waistline and for chopping off heads!

Henry was something of a ladies' man who was suspected to have had half a dozen illegitimate children. He is most famous for having six marriages, and for finding some novel ways to dump his wives. To get rid of his first wife, Catherine of Aragon, because she hadn't delivered a baby boy to succeed him, he clashed with the Roman Catholic Church. They called the religious shots back then and didn't allow divorce, so Henry made himself head of his very own religion—the Church of England. That way, he could divorce her without the permission of the Pope. Easy!

When his second wife, Anne Boleyn, couldn't give him a son either, "Off with her head!" was a very permanent way to end their marriage. (She did, however, have a daughter who would become Queen Elizabeth, who we'll get to shortly).His next wife, Jane Seymour, died in childbirth, although she gave birth to a baby (who became King when he was only nine years old, but who then died when he was only twenty). Henry divorced number four, Anne of Cleves; and then number five, Catherine Howard, also lost her head. His last wife, Catherine Parr, outlived him, surely much to her relief!

Henry was never the same after he was hurt in a jousting accident in 1536. He would stuff his face with food like boars' heads, grilled beavers, and roast swan, and wash that down with plenty of ale. He got so large he could no longer get around and had to be carried by his servants!

MY FOOT HURTS! Bring me a roast swan, two grilled beavers, and a boar's head. That will make me feel much better!

Did you know?

We know how large Henry got because of his armor, which has survived. When he was young, he had a 34-inch (86-cm) waist ... but after his accident he expanded to 52 inches (132 cm).

After that lovely ten course banquet, let's ride off to battle, old Bess!

32 Galileo and the Center of the Universe

Galileo was another of those cool Italian Renaissance men who was part of the scientific revolution going on in the 17th century.

He made his own telescopes to sell to merchant sailors who used them to navigate stormy waters, but Galileo preferred to point his own telescope at the night sky.

Galileo confirmed that the Earth orbited the sun. A clever man called Copernicus had come up with this idea a century before; however, many people at the time were convinced that the Earth was the center of the universe and that everything else circled around it, just as it said in the Bible.

The Pope, however, was not happy. Galileo himself was Catholic, and he knew all too well that the Church would punish people for making such claims against the Bible, perhaps by burning them at the stake or breaking their bodies on a wheel. In the end, Galileo got off lightly and was merely kept under house arrest for the rest of his life.

Did you know?

More than 350 years after the Catholic Church punished Galileo in 1633, Pope John Paul II officially acknowledged in 1992 that Galileo was right and the Earth does indeed orbit the sun. Better late than never, I suppose!

33 Witty Will Shakespeare

While it might sometimes be hard to appreciate William Shakespeare when your teacher asks you to read Hamlet Act 3, Scene I to the class, Will was a real Renaissance man. To this day, he is the most famous writer in the English language—for good reason. He wrote 37 plays, 154 sonnets, and is thought to have introduced 3,000 new words and expressions into the English language. Expressions like "wild goose chase" and "heart of gold" are thanks to him.

Shakespeare wrote famous plays like *Romeo and Juliet* and *Macbeth*, which have been continually performed through history, all over the world, in different languages, and with different interpretations. These plays are supposed to be performed on stage, but if you can't see a live play, a film version can still really bring a play to life. The theater in Will's time was very different to today. There were no women performing in them for starters—the roles of female characters were played by men. The audience also didn't just sit politely and applaud the actors: they would stand, drink, and even boo them!

Shakespeare's children were believed to have been illiterate and some suspicious people even claim that Will was a fraud and that someone else wrote his plays.

Did you know?

Shakespeare, who died in 1616, had a curse written on his gravestone to frighten off potential grave robbers: "Blessed be the man that spares these stones, And cursed be he that moves my bones." It worked a treat—but to this day people remain keen to dig him up to find out more about him!

34   Elizabeth I

Queen Elizabeth I of England, who ruled for 45 years from 1558, is proof that rocking the Renaissance wasn't just a man's game. The daughter of Henry VIII and Anne Boleyn, Elizabeth became the ruler her dad had so desperately wanted to be. She oversaw a golden age in England of stability and exploration, in which people like Shakespeare flourished.

She didn't have it easy, though. When Elizabeth's own sister Mary I became queen, she threw poor Elizabeth in prison in the Tower of London because Mary saw her as a threat. Even when Elizabeth became queen after her sister died, she had trouble with another Mary: her Catholic cousin, Mary Queen of Scots. Elizabeth was a Protestant, and the Catholics were forever hatching plots to put Mary on the throne, so Elizabeth imprisoned Mary to kept an eye on her. When Elizabeth's number one spy, Francis Walsingham—the James Bond of his day—uncovered an assassination plot by Mary, Elizabeth proved she was her father's daughter by having Mary's head cut off!

Elizabeth never married and remained a strong, independent woman to the last. She ruled alone for nearly half a century and did it so well that this period became known through history as the "Golden Age."

I like to think of my dear old dad's advice on dealing with family conflict. OFF WITH HER HEAD!

Did you know?

Elizabeth liked a bit of glamour: she wore thick white makeup that was a mixture of vinegar and lead. We now know that lead can cause a range of skin problems as well as blood-poisoning, so it's best to try this at home!

A little more won't hurt.

35 Witch Trials!

While a renaissance was going on in Europe, not everything was civilized: the 16th and 17th centuries were peak times for putting people on trial for being witches!

A witch was supposedly someone who had made a pact with the devil and was using black magic on people. If anything bad happened in a village, the answer was obvious: it was witches! Any woman who looked a bit old and withered was open to being accused, so lots of poor people were put on trial.

There were some interesting and cruel methods used to test if someone was a witch. One was to strip the accused to their underwear, tie their hands to their feet, and throw them in water. If they floated they were a witch, and if they sank they were innocent—but they most likely drowned!

Another method was to make a "witch cake" out of the urine of the victim who'd been affected by the witch's magic, and then feed it to an animal. If they were a witch, they would apparently cry out in agony.

Anyone unfortunate enough to be found guilty by these methods would find themselves being burnt at the stake or hanged, which hardly seems fair!

Did you know?

Witch trials happened in America too. The Salem Witch Trials between 1692 and 1693 resulted in 20 people being executed —and all because a couple of young girls experienced fits and it was decided that witches were to blame!

Adventures on the High Seas

The Age of Discovery

36 Life on the Ocean Waves

Being a European sailor in the Age of Discovery wasn't for the fainthearted. There was backbreaking work and ships were filthy, damp, and uncomfortable. Columbus had brought back hammocks from the West Indies but they were only beginning to be introduced, so sailors slept on the cold, hard deck, squashed up next to each other.

Food was awful: salted meat and biscuits (not nice ones—more like dry crackers!) were the usual offerings. Salting the food stopped it going bad, but it meant there was a lack of fresh food on long voyages—and that's where the trouble really began.

Nine months at sea fighting sea sickness, home sickness, boredom, and scurvy while sleeping squashed on a hard deck is bad enough! But worse than that... they all snore!

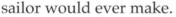

Disease was the biggest problem—especially scurvy. Scurvy is caused by a lack of vitamin C, which comes from fresh fruit and vegetables. You really do need to eat these—it's not just adults saying it! Scurvy causes bleeding gums, stinky breath, tiredness, and spotty skin to start with. Then the sailor's teeth fall out, great boils appear and, yes, you guessed it, that's the last voyage that sailor would ever make.

That was my favorite tooth!

Water was rationed, so sailors could also forget about washing regularly. Sailors drank beer and wine, as it stayed fresh longer than water, although it wouldn't have kept the sailors as focused!

Did you know?

If you were caught breaking the rules aboard a ship, you'd be rewarded with lashes from the cat o' nine tails—basically a multi-stringed whip.

37 Vasco da Gama

Portuguese sailor Vasco da Gama was the first European to sail to India, traveling around Africa in the process.

The reason India was so appealing was simple: spice! The Portuguese king figured that if he could establish a good trading route to India, he could become rich selling the spices. Vasco was just the man to make this happen.

Vasco set off in 1497 and landed in India the following year but he wasn't exactly greeted with open arms. By the time he arrived home, the whole experience was a bit of a disaster, as he had lost half his crew to scurvy.

Da Gama returned to India in 1502 to show off the might of the navy after a Portuguese factory in Calicut (now known as Kozhikode) was destroyed. He caused all sorts of trouble in the region, attacking Calicut and preying on its trade ships in revenge. In 1524, he was named the Portuguese

viceroy of India and asked to return to India again. He got sick not long after arriving back in India, but this was more serious than a case of Delhi belly (diarrhea!): he contracted malaria and there would be no journey home for Vasco.

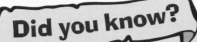

Did you know?

The Portugese were pretty busy on the seas during this time, and they discovered what we now call Brazil. Today, one of the biggest soccer clubs in Rio de Janeiro is named after Vasco da Gama. It's not hard to pick which—the Vasco da Gama soccer club!

38 El Draque

Francis Drake was an English sailor who led the second voyage around the world between 1577 and 1580 in his ship the Golden Hind. (The first was in 1522 by the Spanish: its leader Ferdinand Magellan and most of the sailors were killed during the journey.)

Drake was a hero to the English for beating the Spanish Armada (its navy) when it tried to invade England. He was a pretty relaxed guy. According to legend, he was playing a game of bowls when the Spanish approached, and he made it clear that there was plenty of time to finish his game before fighting the enemy!

However, Drake was also a pirate! The Spanish called him El Draque, and put a massive bounty on his head, with good reason. Drake attacked Spanish ships loaded with gold they'd stolen in the New World and took the treasure back to England. This was much to the delight of Queen Elizabeth I, who had him knighted.

Even his round-the-world voyage was a bit of a pirate cruise, and his biggest capture during the trip was a Spanish ship with 80 pounds (36 kg) of gold and 26 tons of silver. He even found time to land in California and claim it for England!

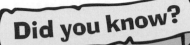

Spanish sailors became so afraid of Drake that they believed he had made a pact with the Devil and had special powers. They thought he had a magic mirror that could help him find treasure ships at sea!

39 Raleigh Adventurous

Sir Walter Raleigh was another English adventurer in the court of Elizabeth I, and he's proof that sometimes it's best to do as you're told!

He was a bit of a teacher's pet: Queen Elizabeth was very fond of him and knighted him. Legend has it that he once laid his expensive cloak over a puddle for Queen Elizabeth to walk over so she wouldn't get her feet wet. What a suck-up!

He wasn't always in the Queen's good books, however. He made her particularly angry by secretly marrying one of her

maids. He was thrown into the Tower of London, which at least gave him some time to indulge one of his other talents: he was a gifted writer, particularly of poetry.

To make things up to the Queen, he followed the Spanish example and went in search of El Dorado (the legendary city of gold) in South America. Needless to say, he never found it, and he wasn't quite so popular with King James I after Elizabeth died. Despite being told to leave the Spanish alone on one of his voyages, he lost his head and attacked them anyway. For that, he literally lost his head in 1618.

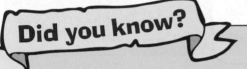

Did you know?

Incredibly for such an adventurer (and, let's face it, a pirate), Raleigh got seasick every time he set sail!

40 The Real Pirates of the Caribbean

With all the gold that the Spanish and Portuguese had plundered from the New World, it was only a matter of time before someone decided to try to pinch it. Enter the pirates!

Real pirates often had official backing from countries like France or England, and were known as "privateers." But for a proper pirate, the most feared on the water during his

time, you need look no further than Blackbeard. With his wide hat, knee-high boots, pistols on a sling, and cutlass, Blackbeard looked like what we think of when we imagine a pirate today, and he flourished during the Golden Age of Piracy at the beginning of the 18th century.

He would light fuses in his long black beard to make him look like a demon as he attacked a ship. Blackbeard used his image to great effect, looting countless ships using fear and intimidation to get what he wanted relatively peacefully (though he could certainly fight when he needed to!). Blackbeard's ship, Queen Anne's Revenge, had 40 guns and a flag that, instead of showing the traditional skull and crossbones, had a skeleton pointing a spear at a bleeding heart. When sailors saw the flag, they'd know it was time to abandon ship!

Blackbeard's luck finally ran out in 1718, when he was killed by British naval officers who defeated him in a surprise attack when he boarded their ship. His head was displayed on the front of their boat, the HMS Pearl, as a warning to other pirates.

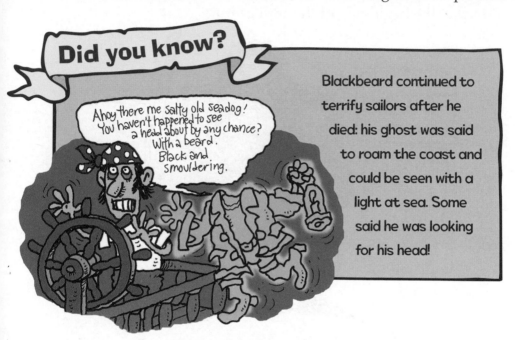

Did you know?

Ahoy there me salty old seadog! You haven't happened to see a head about by any chance? With a beard. Black and smouldering.

Blackbeard continued to terrify sailors after he died: his ghost was said to roam the coast and could be seen with a light at sea. Some said he was looking for his head!

41 Captain Cook

Captain James Cook was a British sailor and explorer who was the first European to land on the east coast of Australia. When he set sail, he hit a bit of a snag when his ship was damaged on the Great Barrier Reef. He repaired his ship where Cooktown in Queensland is today, and he named the river there after his ship, HMS Endeavour!

Cook sailed around New Zealand and mapped its coastline, and he even explored the seas of Antarctica, becoming one of the first Europeans

to sail across the Antarctic Circle. He didn't quite reach Antarctica itself, as it was just too cold for him down there, so he turned back to the sunnier Pacific paradise of Tahiti.

On his final voyage, when he should really have been enjoying his retirement, Cook landed in Hawaii and hung out with the locals. It's thought they initially believed he was some kind of god. It didn't last, however: after an argument with a local chief, he was hit over the head with a club and killed!

Did you know?

Scurvy wasn't much of a factor on Cook's voyages: he had the good sense to stop for fresh supplies and he had some canny, if not exactly yummy, preventions on board, like malt and sauerkraut (fermented cabbage).

Raucous Revolutions

The American and French Revolutions

42 The Boston Tea Party

The Boston Tea Party was proof that if you want to hit the British where it hurts, do it to their favorite drink!

In the 18th century the North-American colonists were still under British rule and were sick and tired of paying high taxes to Britain without having any say in it. So, when ships delivering tea arrived, they were sent away from places like New York, Charleston, and Philadelphia as a protest to the Tea Act—essentially a tax paid on tea brought into the colonies. But a shipment managed to land in Boston.

Trouble was brewing. On December 16, 1773, the Sons of
Liberty (a group formed to protect the rights of the American
colonists) boarded the ships dressed as Native Americans
and committed an act no British person will want to read:
they dumped more than 340 chests of tea into Boston Harbor.
That's around 45 tons (100,000 pounds or over 45,000
kilograms), which would make an awful lot of cups of tea!
This became known as the Boston Tea Party.

The Boston Tea Party was an essentially peaceful protest,
but the British weren't pleased. They closed the port until
the debt was repaid, and passed what the Americans would
come to call the Intolerable Acts (a series of reprisals through

law to try and bring the Americans back under British control), which the Americans felt to be a violation of their rights. If there's one thing Americans value as highly as the British do their tea, it's their rights. Next stop, a revolution!

Did you know?

Many Americans considered drinking tea to be unpatriotic after this incident, so they switched to their new favorite hot drink: coffee.

43 The American War of Independence

Trouble had been simmering for a while between Britain and the Patriots (the Americans that wanted to break away from British-mainland rule). The Patriots wanted independence for the thirteen colonies in North America. The colonies set up their own congress, and in 1775, when fighting broke out, the first gun fired at British soldiers was called the "shot heard around the world." It wasn't really that loud—but its impact was huge!

War broke out, with George Washington as commander in chief of the Patriot forces, known as the Continental Army, against the British and those loyal to them. But Washington had some help from a nation that was in an ongoing war with the British: the French.

At the time, Britain and France really didn't get along. They were always fighting, and had only just finished the Seven Years War with each other in 1763. France originally helped the Patriots secretly, giving them weapons and supplies, but in 1778 they joined the war itself to fight for American independence (and to fight the british some more). Then the Spanish and the Dutch joined up with America too. It seemed like no one liked Britain much!

With Britain certainly having their hands full, in 1783 peace was finally declared with victory for the Patriots. The United States of America was now independent!

Did you know?

Independence Day, on July 4, is a celebration of the Declaration of Independence made in 1776, when the thirteen colonies stated that they were a new nation. People today use "John Hancock" to mean a signature because he signed it in such large letters!

So we've managed to join together as a nation and declare universal human rights and... no one brought a pen?!

44 The First Amercian Presidents

George Washington became the first president of the United States. For his second term, he gave the shortest ever inauguration speech for a US president at only 135 words long (shorter than this page!), which must have been nice for the people there. He made the dollar the currency of America, he wore false teeth made of ivory, and he never actually lived in Washington, D.C.

John Adams was the first president to live in the White House in Washington D.C., and he had a bit of a rivalry

with his vice president Thomas Jefferson, who beat Washington when he tried to get re-elected in 1800. On his deathbed, John said, "Thomas Jefferson survives." Talk about being obsessed with a rival … but it turns out he was actually wrong—Jefferson had died earlier that day— on July 4!

Thomas Jefferson was the third president of the USA—but he didn't even have this written on his gravestone! He was the "man of the people" who was the first president to shake hands with people instead of bowing. He was a real bookworm, and he sold his library to Congress (made up of the Senate and the House of Representatives) in 1815 after theirs had been burned.

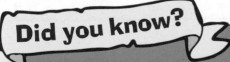

Did you know?

Thomas Jefferson loved books so much that he owned a revolving bookstand so he could have five books open at once!

45 Marie Antoinette

Marie Antoinette was an Austrian princess who enjoyed the good life. She married the French heir to the throne, Louis XVI, when she was only 14, which would certainly be illegal today, and became Queen of France in 1774.

She was the equivalent of a teenage superstar in her day, and she had the lifestyle to go with it. Around 50,000 people turned out to see her at her first public appearance—and some were even crushed to death in the trample to catch a glimpse!

She went to glamorous balls, gambled, and bought lots of clothes and shoes. She loved spending money! This was fine to start with, but France was in a lot of debt after its involvement in the American revolution, and things got out of hand. She used flour to whiten her hair, while the poor didn't have any bread. She had a farming village built at the Palace of Versailles (the palace where the royal family lived) and would dress up as a shepherdess and play the role of a peasant. The French people didn't like the sound of this—

especially when they heard how expensive Versailles was to build. It's estimated it would cost anywhere from two to thirty billion US dollars to build Versailles today!

When the people decided they'd had quite enough, they revolted—and poor Marie lost her head on the guillotine in 1793!

Did you know?

Marie Antoinette made popular the pouf hairstyle, which she wore up to four-feet (1.5- meters) high on her head, often with ostrich feathers. These styles were so high that ladies who copied her would have to kneel down in their carriages to keep it upright!

It's just no good! You'll have to rebuild the doorway so I can get through.

46 The French Revolution

While Americans have Independence Day, the French celebrate July 14 which is when, in 1789, the Bastille prison and armory was stormed by the common people.

The French people were angry at the rising cost of food and at being taxed unfairly to support the lifestyle of the wealthy

and the church. They wanted *liberté, egalité, fraternité* (liberty, equality, fraternity), and they wanted it now. It was time for ordinary people to take the power back!

The people formed a government, making taxes fairer and getting rid of the autocratic powers of their rulers. Panicked, King Louis XVI fled in disguise with his queen Marie Antoinette, but they were recognized near the border. The king clearly hadn't thought about his face being on the country's money! They were captured, France declared itself a republic in 1792, and Louis lost his head on the guillotine in 1793: the new and "more humane" way to behead someone.

However, what should have been a triumph for the people soon turned into a bloody period known as the Terror. Rival revolutionaries fought with each other, extremists took over, and tens of thousands of people were executed by the guillotine.

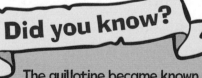

Did you know?

The guillotine became known as the "national razor" in France, and the last person to be executed by it was as recently as 1977.

47 Napoleon

Napoleon was a genius military leader who liked to do things his own way. When he was crowned Emperor of France in 1804 (officially ending the Republic created by the revolution), it was at a glitzy ceremony where he kept the Pope waiting, and then he crowned himself instead of letting anyone else do it!

Napoleon loved a good fight. He spent twelve years fighting the Napoleonic Wars and building a great empire in Europe. Napoleon was not modest about his successes. He had a painting done by a famous portrait painter of the day, Jacques Louis David, of him crossing the Italian alps on a magnificent rearing stallion. In reality, he was not a great rider and crossed the mountains on a mule! Napoleon could definitely get carried away: he led an army into Russia in 1812 and it was a disaster. The freezing winter forced him to retreat

Advance noble steed!

by trudging back through the snow. He lost hundreds of thousands of men, horses, and his artillery in the process.

The game was up for Napoleon in 1814 when he was exiled to the island of Elba in Italy, where life was definitely slower paced, but he missed being involved in the action. He escaped the following year and France welcomed him back with open arms. He got back to doing what he loved: fighting his neighbors.But within 100 days he was crushed at the Battle of Waterloo once and for all. He was sent packing to another island, Saint Helena, which was even more remote, where he eventually died, possibly from boredom.

I've been Emperor of France, created empires in Italy and Africa and am now ruling over all I see... three hundred cockroaches and a mouse.

Did you know?

Napoleon suffered from hemorrhoids (also known as "piles") and his painful behind might have been the reason he was late to launch his attacks at the Battle of Waterloo!

Ask Admiral Nelson if he can give me an extra five minutes. I'm having a few problems here!

TOILET

48 Naughty Nelson

Horatio Nelson, an admiral in the British navy was famous for fighting against the French. He's proof that you can't keep a good man down, as he lost the sight in his right eye during one battle and lost his right arm during another, but still carried on fighting his enemies.

He destroyed the French fleet on the Nile in 1798 when the French were trying to conquer Egypt, which ruined Napoleon's plans there. Despite being on different sides, Horatio and Napoleon had one thing in common: they liked to do things their own way.

Horatio was pretty naughty and he didn't always obey his orders. During the Battle of Copenhagen in 1801, when he was told to stop his attacks, he looked through his telescope with his blind eye and pretended he couldn't see the order so he could carry on!

Those Danes haved turned off all the lights over there in Copenhagen. All I can see is black!

Horatio went out with a bang. During his last voyage at the Battle of Trafalgar, despite being outnumbered and outgunned, he launched a daring attack and beat the combined French and Spanish fleet without losing a single ship. But in the process, he was shot in the shoulder by a French sniper, which was finally enough to finish him off.

Did you know?

As he lay dying, Nelson is believed to have said to his friend Captain Hardy, "Kiss me, Hardy." Proof that even tough guys can have tender moments!

49 The Iron Duke

Known as the Iron Duke, Arthur Wellesley was the Duke of Wellington and the man famous for putting a stop to Napoleon at the Battle of Waterloo in 1815. But his forces didn't do it alone. They had help from Prussian (German) allies led by Gebhard Leberecht von Blücher.

Napoleon and the Duke were certainly a bit two-faced with each other. Napoleon would say nasty things publicly about the Duke but nice things about him privately, while the Duke preferred to praise the Frenchman publicly and insult Napoleon behind his back. They finally got to settle their differences on the battlefield. On the day of Waterloo, Napoleon said that Wellington was a bad general and France would win easily. Embarrassing!

Once victory was his, Wellington made sure that Napoleon wasn't executed. Don't mistake the Iron Duke for being too soft though: he rubbed salt into the wounds of his enemy by going out with two of Napoleon's ex-girlfriends!

As for Napoleon, his feelings about the Duke were made clear after he died. He left some money in his will for a man who had tried to assassinate the Iron Duke!

Did you know?

Napoleon commissioned a huge statue of himself, where he was naked except for a fig leaf over his private parts. When Napoleon was defeated, Wellington had the statue put in his house. Definitely an original decorative choice!

The Age of Empires

The British and European Empires

50 Convict Island

It might seem hard to imagine, but living in Australia was once considered a punishment. The country was a penal colony, which basically meant it was a prison!

British ships landed in 1788 where we now call Sydney, and the majority of people onboard were convicts. They weren't all particularly hardened criminals. Some of them were children, and many had committed only minor crimes: one woman had done nothing more than steal a bit of cheese!

The journey from England to Australia took eight months, and the conditions on the ships were unpleasant. The convicts were kept below deck, which was hot and humid. There were also plenty of creepy crawlies, which might have been good training for the country they were going to, considering its reputation for snakes, spiders, and other bugs! Bedbugs, lice, and cockroaches were everywhere, and it's estimated that 48 people died on the journey—which was considered a small number at the time!

The new settlers struggled. Farming was tough, and they had to survive on dwindling rations that were topped up by incoming British boats. No wonder Australia was considered

a suitable prison: who needs bars and chains when you're hundreds of miles from the nearest country and there's nothing but blazing-hot bush around?

During the early years in the colonies in Australia, rum was used as currency instead of coins or notes!

51 Aboriginal Australians

When the British turned up in Australia, the indigenous Aboriginal people didn't feel like the country was a prison. It was their home, after all. Aboriginal Australians have lived in Australia for more than 40,000 years! But that didn't matter to the settlers. They decimated the indigenous population through diseases like smallpox, and with their weapons: an Aboriginal spear was a pretty poor answer to a rifle.

However, the Aborigines had learned to live in the harsh conditions, unlike the colonists, and to use cool tools like the boomerang to hunt animals. A boomerang is a wooden tool that is designed to spin through the air and club a hunted animal, rather than impale it like a spear would. This means that a boomerang doesn't have to be thrown with as great as accuracy as a spear and also covers a wider area with each throw. Some boomerangs are curved at the ends and are designed to return to the thrower if they miss their target.

When Aboriginal kids were between the age of 10 and 16, they had to go off on "walkabout," which means going off to live in the wilderness for a few months to live off the land and make the spiritual journey into becoming an adult. Would you be able to handle a few months in the bush on your own with nothing but your wits to protect you? Didn't think so!

Did you know?

Australia Day is celebrated on January 26 which was the date in 1788 when the first colonizers arrived. For many Aboriginal and Torres Strait Islander people, however, it is a day of mourning that many call "Invasion Day" or "Survival Day."

52 Queen Victoria

In 1837, at the age of 18, Victoria became Queen and ruled the vast British Empire for over 60 years. She married her cousin Albert in 1840: she proposed to him, which was definitely ahead of its time, although to be fair, he wasn't allowed to propose to her because she was queen!

They had nine children, which became handy later when they started pairing them up to marry members of royal families all over Europe. There's no alliance like a family alliance! Albert, however, died in 1861, and Queen Victoria was so sad that she wore black for the rest of her life.

She was a popular queen: a whole era was even named after her (the Victorian era), as well as places all around the world,

such as the state of Victoria in Australia, the city of Victoria in Canada, and Victoria Falls in Africa. But that didn't stop some people wanting to put a stop to her! There were several assassination attempts, with the preferred method being to fire a pistol at her carriage. Some would-be assassins were declared insane while one was given what some considered a fate worse than death: being sent to Australia for a lifetime of hard labor!

Did you know?

Queen Vic was the first British monarch to live at Buckingham Palace. A teenager known as "the boy Jones" repeatedly broke in and was caught stealing her underwear!

53 Indian Rebellion

The British East India Company was a vital part of the British Empire's dealings with the East, trading in things like cotton and Britain's favorite drink, tea. The East India Company had been at the heart of a trade war with China, the great tea-growing country. Then in 1857, the people of India decided that they'd had quite enough of being ruled by a trading company!

Some Indian soldiers in the army rebelled and killed their commanding officers, and then they encouraged their fellow Indians to go on a brutal rampage, which came as a bit of a shock to the British. But not for long. They soon went on a brutal rampage of their own.

The British eventually stopped the rebellion, got rid of the East India Company and ruled the country directly: a period known as the British Raj, when India was the jewel of the crown in the British Empire. They also started to listen to the Indian people a little more and gave more respect to their traditions and customs, chief of which involved stopping trying to force Christianity upon them and overthrowing Indian nobles who didn't agree with them. They maybe should have thought not to do that in the first place!

THE EAST INDIA COMPANY

CLOSED!

TEA TEA
TEA TEA
TEA
TEA

Oh how disappointing! I've just spent an uncomfortable ride from the Punjab by elephant for a packet of English Breakfast tea and they're closed!

Did you know?

The British did a lot of harm in India, but one thing they did put a stop to was a form of execution where a condemned man would be trampled to death by an elephant.

54 The Scramble for Africa

Up until the late 19th century, few of the European powers hadn't shown much interest in Africa beyond enslaving people to send out to the New World. By now, however, most of Europe had abolished slavery. This came in handy once the mad scramble was underway to start colonizing Africa, because Europe could use "ridding the continent of slavery" as an excuse to do it! Bringing Christianity and its so-called "civilizing" influence on the continent was another excuse. In reality, power and material goods were the reasons! France had already invaded Algeria, but it was King Leopold II of Belgium who, spying an opportunity to cash in on the great natural resources in the Congo (such as rubber), really got things started. Once he claimed it, it was time for the other European powers to… SCRAMBLE!

Britain took plenty of the continent, including Egypt and South Africa, which were vital to its route to India. The French conquered much of west Africa and the Germans and Portuguese claimed parts of the continent too. With the empires' industrial technology and weaponry, the lands weren't particularly difficult to conquer and they were more than happy to bleed these new lands (and their people) dry for their own gain.

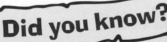

Did you know?

Henry Stanley was an explorer and journalist who trekked deep into Africa to find missing British missionary David Livingstone. When he found him, Stanley delivered the ice-cool line: "Dr. Livingstone, I presume?"

Fierce Frontiers

The American and Canadian West, and the Australian Bush

55 Gold Rush!

In 1848, gold was found in California, and where there's gold there are sure to be people chasing it! The thousands of people who moved there in 1849 to try to strike it rich became known as the "49ers." You might notice a certain San Francisco NFL (National Football League) team is named after these prospectors.

Some people got very lucky—and very rich. Most people, however, didn't. It was the merchants who followed them

who struck gold in a very different sense, as they had lots of customers. San Francisco grew from a small town to an important city, with parts of it built on abandoned sunken ships. In 1850, California became the 31st state of the USA.

JEREMIAH THE PROSPECTOR'S WORST KEPT SECRET OF 1849

In 1851 in Australia, there it was again: GOLD RUSH! People traveled from all over the country, and then from all over the world in search of the shiny stuff. Britain was coming to the end of sending its prisoners there, which was probably just as well, given there might have been a crime spree with people desperate for a free ride to the gold rush.

Some say the diggers' collective defiance of authority and embracing of friendship is where the Aussie character comes

from, but how far would those friendships have stretched if they'd found one of the giant gold nuggets that a region like Victoria was famous for?

Did you know?

Levi Strauss was one of the merchants who struck it rich during the gold rush when he co-patented a pair of strengthened work pants. These were the first example of what we know know as jeans and his company 'Levi's jeans' still exists today.

56 The American Civil War

The industrial Northern states of America wanted to end slavery, but the more rural Southern states were against the idea, as they used slave labor on their cotton and tobacco plantations. When Abraham Lincoln was elected president

in 1860 and the Southern way of life became threatened, 11 Southern states broke away to form their own country. It seemed that there was only one way to settle it: fight!

The American Civil War (1861–65) was the bloodiest war in the country's history. The Southern side were called the Confederates, and the Northerners were called the Union. After a bad start for the North, Abraham Lincoln made the Emancipation Proclamation, which meant the war wasn't just about preserving the Union anymore—it was about freeing the slaves too.

General Robert E. Lee was a brilliant military commander for the South, winning great battles even when outnumbered, but he was a bit too aggressive for his own good. He invaded

the North, which was a gutsy move ... until he spectacularly lost the Battle of Gettysburg in 1863, during which 3000 union soldiers ended up facing 60,000 advancing Confederate soldiers.

In 1865, after a brutal invasion by the Union, the Confederates finally admitted defeat, with the South in ruins.

Did you know?

Stonewall Jackson was a great Southern general who played a big part in the South's famous victory at the Battle of Chancellorsville. But he was accidentally shot by his own men during it!

57 Abraham Lincoln

Abe Lincoln was the legendary American president who proved that if at first you don't succeed, try, try, and try again!

Lincoln failed in all sorts of things, from business to being nominated for vice president, but he eventually succeeded in getting the top job of president in 1860, and he made sure he left his mark on history.

He came from a poor background, but taught himself law. He earned himself the nickname "Honest Abe," which not many lawyers could do! As president, his Gettysburg Address became one of the most famous speeches ever, he led the Union in the Civil War, and he helped to abolish slavery.

Lincoln was a giant, standing at 6 foot 4 inches (193 cm) tall, (which was particularly tall in those days). With his stovepipe hat and full beard, he was certainly hard to miss. In 1864, someone shot at him … but only hit his hat, which was a close shave!

In the end, unfortunately, he proved a little harder to miss. On April 14, 1865, only five days after the surrender of the South in the American Civil War, Lincoln was shot in the head and killed while at the theater by Confederate (and actor) John Wilkes Booth. He wasn't wearing his hat at the time!

Did you know?

Lincoln was a handy wrestler who was honored by the National Wrestling Hall of Fame in America. He competed in around 300 matches over 12 years and only lost once!

58 Ned Kelly

Ned Kelly was an Australian bushranger (the equivalent of an outlaw in the American West) who became a folk hero as a symbol of rebellion against authority.

He was always brave and was awarded a green sash when he was a child for saving another boy from drowning in a creek. He was often crossing paths with the law too; he got into trouble for stealing some money when he was only 14. He soon progressed to horses, and then to banks, and eventually to murder!

When he was accused by a policeman (who was later proven to be a bit of a liar) of shooting at him, Ned and his gang hid out in a place called the Wombat Ranges. When the police came looking for them, Ned shot three dead, and his gang became WANTED: DEAD OR ALIVE.

The Kelly gang had their last stand in Glenrowan in 1880. They wore iron armor, looking a bit like Aussie knights, but it had one fatal weakness: the armor didn't cover their legs! The police aimed low and shot one of the gang in his groin – ow! Ned was shot in the legs and captured, and when he was hanged for his sins, legend has it that his last words were, "Such is life."

Did you know?

Ned's skeleton has been found, but his skull is missing. A skull found in a plastic container was believed to be the one, but tests proved otherwise. The search continues!

59 The Great Plains

Native Americans believed that the land didn't belong to anybody. Unfortunately, that was not the stance of the land-grabbing Europeans when they colonized the country.

The way of life of many of the famous tribes of the Great Plains, like the Cheyenne, Comanche, Blackfoot, and Plains Apache, was based around the buffalo. They hunted buffalo and ate their livers raw, and made clothes and teepees out of the skins. They even made fires using dried buffalo poop!

The tribes were constantly on the move, taking their teepees with them as they moved around the Great Plains following the animals. When war broke out with the colonizers, the Europeans hunted the buffalo for sport and to starve the tribes.

Native Americans believed in the power of spirits, and they held ceremonies to please them. They performed the Sun Dance, where the dancers faced spiritual and physical tests for the good of their people, and which was outlawed by the European colonizers—a ban that was only lifted as recently as the 1970s.

Respecting the elders in the tribe was important, which is something we all should do—yes, even respecting teachers!

Did you know?

Crazy Horse, a Lakota warrior and leader, didn't always have such a cool name. When he was young, he was nicknamed "Curly" because of his curly hair. He had a vision of himself riding into battle on a horse and told his father about it, who decided it was time for a new name.

60 The Battle of the Little Bighorn

The settlers discovered gold in the Black Hills in the USA (a mountain range which stretches from South Dakota into Wyoming) which meant that they were very keen to mine the mountains. But there was one major obstacle: the Native Americans who had been living on that land for thousands of years. Unfortunately, once gold gets in the sights of greedy settlers, there's usually no stopping them.

When some of the Native Americans decided that they wouldn't move off the land into reservations just so white folk could have the land, thank you very much, the US president declared any Native Americans who didn't comply were "hostiles." It was fighting time once again.

Sitting Bull was the leader of a group of these "hostiles," and George Custer of the American cavalry, who had led the expedition that started the gold rush in the first place, was about to find out just how hostile they could be! When he led his soldiers into the Little Bighorn valley in 1876, he was like someone who hadn't studied for a test: totally unprepared. There were many, many more Native Americans than he expected, and Custer, who'd had good luck in his battles, finally saw his luck run out. Afterwards, for good measure, the Native Americans scalped a lot of the US troops.

"Follow me men! Let's get this Battle of the Little Bighorn over and done with and be home by lunchtime."

Did you know?

Custer finished bottom of his class at military school and, while some people think the battle was a glorious and brave "last stand" by Custer, plenty of others think his arrogance and blunders were to blame for the defeat.

61 The Mounties

In 1867, Canada became a country made up of its British colonies, and six years later one of its most famous institutions was started: the Mounties, or the Royal Canadian Mounted Police.

Riding horses and wearing red tunics and distinctive hats, the Mounties are instantly recognizable, which isn't always a good thing if the bad guys can see them coming!

One of their first tasks was to clamp down on the illegal whiskey trade. They spent months marching west over harsh Canadian terrain and facing hostilities from local people on the way, to the aptly named Fort Whoop-Up, where the whiskey traders were based. Once the Mounties arrived, the party was well and truly over!

Sitting Bull, the Native American leader of the group who cut Custer and his men down to size at Little Bighorn, went to Canada to escape the Americans, who wanted revenge. He ran into the Mounties, and formed a friendship with one of them, James Walsh, who became a strong defender of Sitting Bull and his people. You can always rely on a Mountie!

Did you know?

The famous Mountie hat didn't become an official part of the uniform until around the turn of the 20th century, when it replaced the traditional white pith helmet.

62 Jesse James

Jesse James was one of the most famous outlaws of the American West, but before that Jesse was a Confederate soldier in the American Civil War who was shot in the chest ... but survived!

Jesse and his gang were wanted for robbing banks and trains. During a robbery in 1869, Jesse shot a cashier for revenge, as he believed the man had killed his friend during the Civil War. But, Jesse had got the wrong guy!

Jesse wrote letters to the *Kansas City Times* newspaper to print, which painted him as a Confederate hero and a bit of a Robin Hood, stealing from the rich to give to the poor. It wasn't true, of course. His gang stole from the banks and gave the money to themselves!

It had to come to an end eventually: in 1882, fellow gang member Bob Ford betrayed Jesse by shooting him in the back of the head while he was hanging a picture. He could at least have waited until he'd got it straight! Bob toured the country performing a stage show of his murderous act, but eventually a tough critic used a gun to bring the curtain down on him for good in 1892.

Did you know?

Some people had doubts that it was really Jesse James who had been killed. To settle it once and for all, his body was dug up in 1995 to make sure. It was him all right.

Of course it's really me!

63 Gunfight at the O.K. Corral

The Gunfight at the O.K. Corral is one of the most famous incidents of the American West – and it only lasted about 30 seconds!

The fight took place in the aptly named mining town of Tombstone, Arizona, on October 26, 1881. On one side stood local lawmen Wyatt Earp and his two brothers, along with legendary gambler, gunfighter, and dentist—yes, dentist—Doc Holliday. On the other stood the Clanton brothers and the McLaury brothers: they were called "cowboys," which was considered an insult at the time, as it meant cattle rustlers.

Welcome to TOMBSTONE Arizona Home of the Gunfight at the O.K. CORRAL

The great myths and movies of the Old West paint this fight as the good guys versus the bad guys, but as always with history, the truth isn't so clear! In fact, Wyatt Earp and his men were just as bad as their opponents. It's likely that they fired first, at point-blank range, and that some of the "bad guys" weren't even armed. That didn't happen in the movies!

By the time the dust had settled and some 30 shots had been fired, the McLaury brothers and one of the Clanton brothers were dead, while the other Clanton, who was unarmed, had done the smart thing and run away!

Did you know?

Wyatt Earp later became a boxing referee, and he was accused of fixing a big fight that he refereed in 1896. During his lifetime, he was more famous for this infamous accusation than for his role in the O.K. Corral!

Lightbulb Moments

Amazing Inventions and the Industrial Age

64 The Industrial Revolution

The Industrial Revolution of the 18th and 19th centuries saw the world change dramatically, thanks to the introduction of steam power and new machines and technologies. These advances would bring great improvements to society, unless you were unfortunate enough to work in one of the factories or mines at the time!

Working conditions were terrible, with 14-hour shifts and low pay expected of employees. People worked in filthy, dangerous conditions, using early forms of machinery without any of the

safety measures we have today, so lots of workers ended up in hospital with injuries. And don't think being a child got you off the hook—children were expected to work too. They'd have to climb into dangerous machinery to clean it and go deep into horrible mines, all for lower pay than adults. Plus, if children did anything wrong, they were beaten by their boss or even had weights tied around their necks as punishment. Maybe now school doesn't seem so bad after all!

Living conditions weren't much better. You might have to share a room with lots of other tired, dirty people from the factory. Rubbish was just thrown on the street, there weren't always toilet facilities, and there were open sewers. Cities absolutely stank – and there'd also be plenty of disease, like cholera, which came from dirty water. Yuck!

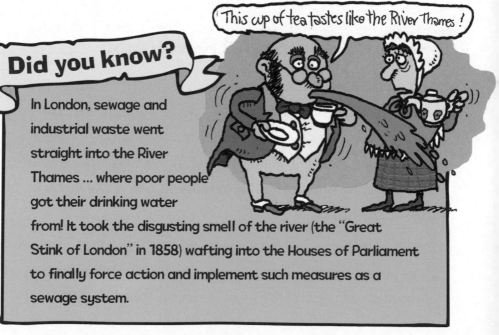

Did you know?

This cup of tea tastes like the River Thames!

In London, sewage and industrial waste went straight into the River Thames ... where poor people got their drinking water from! It took the disgusting smell of the river (the "Great Stink of London" in 1858) wafting into the Houses of Parliament to finally force action and implement such measures as a sewage system.

65 Toilet Paper

Sure, now there's usually toilet paper there on the roll for us after we've finished our business, but it wasn't always so!

While the ancient Romans had sponges to wipe their bottoms, the Greeks were quite keen on using stones, though preferably smooth ones, and you'd need a pile of them just in case!

Other wiping methods have been used over the years, ranging from the obvious, like leaves, to the less obvious, such as the cobs from corn on the cob! Hopefully that won't put you off eating your corn. Some people even just used their hand!

The Chinese were producing toilet paper in bulk during the 14th-century Ming Dynasty, and they'd been using it for centuries before that, so they got there long before the West caught up. Joseph Gayetty was the man to do it in America: his toilet paper was first introduced in 1857. And this wasn't just any cheap old paper that you might find in your school toilets: this stuff was scented and watermarked with its maker's initials on the paper. Classy!

Did you know?

Gayetty's toilet paper was originally marketed as an aid to people suffering from piles (hemorrhoids). Ouch!

66 Black Gold

Oil is the black gold that has made many people rich: it's a substance we simply can't seem to get enough of, as we use it in our cars, airplanes, and industry, which is a bit of a shame, as one day it will run out!

Edwin "Crazy" Drake was the first man to successfully drill for oil in America in 1859. Drake was a wildcatter, which was the name given to people who drilled hoping to strike oil. As for why he was nicknamed "Crazy," well, he was simply obsessed with finding oil, and he spent months trying before he finally did. Although he was the first to extract oil properly, he didn't patent his methods; he wound up penniless and bitter while others made their fortunes from oil.

I knew if I drilled absolutely everywhere I'd eventually strike oil!

One such man had a name you might be familiar with: J.D. Rockefeller. He set up the Standard Oil Company of Ohio in 1870, and used some interesting methods in his business, including hiring spies to get the lowdown on his competitors! When he retired 27 years later, he was the richest man in America – worth one billion dollars. That's an incredible amount of money today, but back then it was unthinkable!

Did you know?

Rockefeller's son, the imaginatively named J.D. Rockefeller Junior, was the man behind the world-famous Rockefeller Center in New York City.

67 The Light Bulb

American inventor Thomas Edison was one of the leading lights of his time. He helped bring electricity into people's homes, had over a thousand patents in his name, and is the man we must thank for the electric light bulb. Edison didn't actually invent the light bulb, but he was the first to come up with a useable version of it in 1879. After all, what good is a light that doesn't work? His first model only lasted a few hours before the bulb died, which wouldn't be much use if your homework was due the next day! But he got much, much better at it.

He didn't always get it right, and he wasn't above having feuds with rivals. Another ace inventor, Nikola Tesla, who sported a striking mustache, came up with a better way of

transmitting electricity … but Edison simply said, "Thanks, but no thanks!" But when Tesla took it to Edison's rival George Westinghouse, the War of the Currents began. It obviously wasn't a real war, but it did see Edison get a bit nasty. He said his rivals' alternating current was the best way to execute a criminal in the electric chair and, horrifically, he tested it on dogs to prove his point!

As well as the lightbulb, Edison also invented the phonograph, which allowed him to record and play back sounds, and an early motion-picture camera.

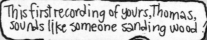

This first recording of yours, Thomas, sounds like someone sanding wood!

That's not a recording! I'm just sanding rough edges off the phonograph!

68 Lady Liberty

The Statue of Liberty is one of the most famous structures in the world, and it was often the first sight people were greeted with when they emigrated to the USA.

France planned to present the the statue to the USA in 1876, as a gift to celebrate the centennial of the Declaration of Independence, and this date is inscribed on her torch. Frédéric Auguste Bartholdi designed it and Gustave Eiffel—the man

behind the Eiffel Tower in Paris—helped build it. It was completed in 1886, so 10 years late!

The statue was built in France and then shipped over to the USA to be constructed. When the head was finished, Lady Liberty was exhibited at the Paris World's Fair in 1878—minus her body! The whole statue was made up of over 300 pieces that were packed up and shipped to America, although the ship almost sank in stormy seas!

While the statue was a gift, the base had to be paid for by the people of New York. They had trouble raising the cash, but eventually got there with a very early form of crowdfunding (where a large group fund a project by each donating a small amount). When it first arrived, it was the tallest structure in New York. It wasn't always the light-green color we are familiar with today: it was a bright copper color, as that's the material that Lady Liberty is coated in. The green color is the result of the copper weathering over time.

Did you know?

The Statue of Liberty can sway up to 3 inches (almost 8 cm) in 50 mph (80 kmh) winds. When Hurricane Sandy struck in 2012, the statue was closed for months, but Lady Liberty was fine—it was the damage around her that cost millions to repair!

69 The Wright Stuff

Today, if we're fortunate enough, we can fly almost anywhere we want to in the world, so it's hard to believe that it wasn't until 1903 that the first powered aircraft took flight.

The Wright brothers were bicycle-shop owners in Dayton, Ohio, in the USA. They tested gliders before taking on the challenge of building the first airplane. They built a brand-new engine to power a biplane (a plane with two wings, one on top of the other) with a propeller. The brothers, Wilbur and Orville, tossed a coin to see who would have first go. Wilbur won and took the controls … only to stall the plane and crash it. D'oh!

Once they'd fixed it, Orville decided to show his brother how it was done. He took off successfully and made history with the first flight that lasted a dazzling 12 seconds and traveled 120 feet (36 meters). You'd be better off walking! By the end of the day, Wilbur had a go too and the plane flew further and further.

The Wrights had plenty of rivals, and one of them, Glenn Curtiss, piloted a rival plane made by former Smithsonian Institution secretary Samuel P. Langley and the institution exhibited it as the first plane "capable of flight." This angered the Wrights so much that they refused to give their historical plane to the Smithsonian, donating it to a science museum all the way in London instead!

Did you know?

That's one small step for man, one giant flight for the Wright brothers.

When Neil Armstrong became the first man on the moon 66 years later, he did so with a piece of fabric from the Wright brothers' first airplane in his pocket. Now that's flying!

70 Radioactive!

Marie Curie was an amazing scientist who, in 1903, was the first woman to win a Nobel Prize. She was so good, in fact, that she won two – her second coming in 1911. With her husband, Pierre, she discovered two new chemical elements: polonium (which she named after the country of her birth, Poland) and radium. She came up with the concept of "radioactivity," and was even friends with Albert Einstein.

During the Curies' incredible research, Marie only really made one mistake, but it was a costly one! No one knew the harmful effects of radioactive

substances at the time, so she happily handled them without any kind of protection, cheerfully keeping radioactive test tubes in her pocket and on her desk, enjoying the fact that they glowed in the dark. Uh oh...

Marie was a principled woman and didn't believe she should patent or profit from radium, but others sold it in all sorts of forms. A cure for hair loss! A laxative to make you go to the toilet! A whitening toothpaste!

This meant that people were actually brushing their teeth with radioactive material! Luckily for most, the sellers lacked the skill to use radium as Marie had, but poor Marie paid for it when she died at the age of 66 from exposure to radiation.

Darling, do you think that new radium toothpaste and hair restorer I bought from the store are starting to do their thing?

Did you know?

The papers Marie Curie wrote in the 1890s are still too radioactive to handle safely, as is her cookbook, though hopefully there are no recipes involving radium in there!

71 Beep! Beep!

If you get dropped off at school each morning by your parents, it's easy to take cars for granted—but it wasn't always like this.

It wasn't until 1885 that the first motor car hit the roads (not that they had a great road network then!), thanks to German engineer Karl Benz (you may recognize his surname from Mercedes-Benz). His Motorwagen car was a petrol-powered three-wheeler that you wouldn't be seen dead in today, but without it you might still be walking to school!

These old cars had to be started with a hand crank instead of a key, which could make starting the car on a cold morning really hard work! Karl's wife, Bertha, took the kids out for a 60-mile (96-km) spin in the Motorwagen to prove how good it was.

Given that its top speed was 6 miles per hour (9.6 km/h, which is just a bit faster than walking pace), you can only hope that none of the kids asked, "Are we there yet?"

Benz improved his design in later years, adding an extra wheel to make four, but it was Henry Ford who really made the motor car popular in America. His Model T, first made in 1908, was affordable and became the first car to be made on a factory assembly line—so thousands could be made in a week!

Did you know?

The world's first speeding ticket was given to a man named Walter Arnold in England in 1896. He was doing 8 mph (13 kmh) in a 2-mph (3.2-kmh) zone ... and the officer who stopped him was riding a bicycle!

72 Albert Einstein

Take the smartest kid in your class, multiply their mind power by a thousand and you still won't get close to perhaps the biggest brain of them all—German scientist Albert Einstein.

Einstein's work in physics changed the world. It's thanks to him that we have things like GPS (good luck using online maps without it!), super-accurate clocks, lasers, and our knowledge of things like the Big Bang and black holes. On the other hand, his work indirectly helped create the atom bomb, and if you've ever struggled with the equation $E=mc^2$ (part of his famous theory of relativity) in science class, well, you have him to blame for that!

Einstein wasn't even a full-time scientist when he started—he worked as a patent clerk and published his papers in his spare time. In his later years, with his big mustache, messy hair, and moth-eaten sweaters, he looked exactly how we imagine a "nutty professor" would!

When Adolf Hitler came to power in 1933, Einstein, who was Jewish, quite rightly thought he'd be better off in the USA. When he heard that the Nazis were trying to make an atomic bomb, he urged the Americans to do the same, though once the bomb had been used he regretted it, as he was strongly opposed to conflict and war. He also supported civil rights, so naturally the FBI in America spent years tapping his phone and going through his trash. They were worried Einstein might be a Russian spy as well as a great scientist!

Did you know?

Einstein wanted to be cremated after he passed away, but when he died, someone first took his brain away to try to discover the secret of his genius! in 2012 it was discovered, among other things, that Einstein actually had an extra ridge on his mid-frontal lobe—which is the part of the brain used for making plans and working memory—he had four rather than the usual three.

73 The "Unsinkable" Ship

The *RMS Titanic* was the biggest ship ever built back in 1912, at 880 feet (269 meters) long and 175 feet (53 meters) high, which allowed the room for the 3,000 people onboard. The ship was called "unsinkable" before its first voyage, so what happened? It sank, of course!

The *Titanic* hit an iceberg in the Atlantic Ocean; within three hours the ship broke in two and was at the bottom of the sea, which was enough time for plenty of mistakes to be made. The biggest of these had been made before leaving: there were only enough lifeboats for about a third of the people onboard. Oops! And when the first lifeboat was put in the water, it wasn't even half full. Double oops!

There were enough life jackets onboard, but they were of little use, given that the water was below freezing point. You

really wouldn't want to be swimming in that! Tragically, some 1,500 people died. The policy was women and children first on the lifeboats, so one ice-cool cat and his valet changed into their best clothes and sat on deckchairs drinking brandy and smoking cigars as they went down with the ship.

ICEBERG SIR!

Did you know?

There may not have been enough room for all the people on the lifeboats, but three dogs made it off alive! They were little dogs, though, so they didn't take up a seat.

I don't know about you but I'm glad to get off that ship!

TITANIC

War, What is it Good for? (Part 1)

World War I

74 Terrible Trenches

World War I kicked off in the summer of 1914, with the Allies on one side (Britain, France, Russia, and Serbia, and the USA joining in 1917) and the Central Powers of Germany, Austria-Hungary and the Ottoman Empire (Turkey) on the other. Both sides thought it would be over by Christmas … but it lasted four years. Most of this time was spent in a stalemate at the Western Front, where each side had a line of trenches facing

each other that ran across France and Belgium, from the North Sea to the Swiss border. Each side was trying to gain more of the other's territory. The Front didn't move more than 10 miles (16 km) in either direction for three years. Now that's slow progress!

The muddy trenches were absolutely filthy. There were dead bodies, overflowing toilets, and giant rats. There weren't exactly brilliant bathing facilities either, so people were dirty and riddled with lice, which would make them itchy and cause the horrible "trench fever."

Good luck getting any sleep, because in some places you were only 50 yards (46 meters) from the enemy trench. The area between the trenches was called No Man's Land, and soldiers dreaded the order to go "over the top," which meant climbing out of the trench and running toward the enemy, who were armed to the teeth with machine guns and artillery. Refusing the order meant you'd be shot by your own men, making it not much of a choice at all!

Did you know?

Around 250,000 underage boys (the age limit was 19) lied about their age to join the British army and fight in the war. Would you fancy signing up to life in the trenches?

75 Soccer Match

During Christmas of 1914, the war at the Front actually stopped for a very brief moment. A Christmas truce was called in the trenches, which was against the orders given to the soldiers, but then sometimes it's good not to do what we're told!

The Germans had beer and Christmas trees and on Christmas Eve they sang "Silent Night" … and the British soldiers joined in! The soldiers started shouting messages to each other about maybe having a day off from all that senseless shooting and killing. It was Christmas, after all.

On Christmas Day, it was eerily quiet. Officers from each side met in No Man's Land and it was agreed that there'd be a truce for Christmas. The soldiers, who had been firing at each other just the day before, came out and said hello to their enemies. The Germans gave the Brits beer and the Brits shared their plum pudding. Soccer matches were played in No Man's Land, though not really according to the rules of the game!

If you think the day after Christmas is disappointing after the excitement of the day before, imagine how the poor soldiers must have felt in 1914 when the fighting started again!

Did you know?

One German soldier definitely not getting into the Christmas spirit was a young corporal by the name of Adolf Hitler, who told his fellow soldiers off for talking of a truce!

76 Gallipoli

World War I was bad news for some of Britain's colonies, as it meant they had to fight too.

The Anzacs (the Australian and New Zealander troops) in particular were involved in the Gallipoli campaign of 1915 when, because of the stalemate at the trenches on the Front, the Allies decided they'd capture Constantinople (which is Istanbul in Turkey today), the capital of the crumbling Ottoman Empire.

Gallipoli was an absolute disaster. The Allies thought it would be such a walkover that they brought old ships and had

little in the way of maps or intelligence. Their commanders hesitated and made blunders. They landed from the sea, with the Anzacs at one end of the beach and the British at the other, but some of the battleships hit mines and sank, and when the soldiers finally landed, they didn't get much further than the beach!

Things soon became familiar, as trench warfare started up once again—the very thing the Allies had hoped to avoid. It would last nearly a year. On the bright side, when they finally admitted defeat and retreated, they did so splendidly. They tricked the Ottomans into thinking they weren't running away at all but were attacking, until it was too late for the Ottomans to do anything about the retreat.

> ### Did you know?
>
> The British political leader of the navy, Winston Churchill, was blamed for the Gallipoli failure and was demoted for it. "I'm finished!" he said, but of course he wasn't—he'd be back for World War II!

77 The Red Baron

Airplanes featured in a major conflict for the first time during World War I, and no pilot was more fearsome than the legendary German knight of the sky: Manfred von Richthofen, known as the Red Baron!

No mere biplane would do for the Red Baron, so he flew a bright red triplane instead, the sight of which let the Allies know that they were in for a really bad day. He downed 80 enemy planes, including some of the top flying aces, and he led a gang of fighter-pilot buddies known as the Flying Circus.

My mother, Frau von Richthofen, told me to paint my plane blue like the sky. But I chose bright red. It'll be the death of me she said.

The pilots fought in the air in what were called "dog fights," but which (obviously) didn't involve any animals! At the start of the war, the pilots fired at each other with handheld revolvers. Machine guns were later added to the planes once they'd figured out how to stop shooting their own propellers off!

What goes up, however, must come down in the end. No pilot could quite match the Red Baron, but he finally went down in 1918. He was shot by an Australian gunner on the ground, though the British air force credited a Canadian pilot with the kill, and plenty of other claims have been put forward!

Did you know?

At the start of the war, when planes were used mainly for reconnaissance, pilots often got lost and had to land to ask for directions!

I say there chaps! I think I'm a tad lost. It would be jolly good if you could point me in the direction of England thanks! I must be home for tea.

78 Russian Revolution(s)

Things weren't going well in Russia during World War I. Millions of people had been either captured or killed and there was a shortage of food. It hadn't helped that Tsar Nicholas II, who wasn't the brightest, had taken control of the military himself. This was a bad idea for the war effort and a terrible one for the country, as he left his wife Alexandra in charge. She was influenced by a man called Grigori Rasputin, known as the "mad monk," who had some very strange beliefs and was very unpopular. So unpopular, in fact, that he was murdered in 1916.

In February 1917, thousands of workers went on strike and people took to the streets demanding bread. The army was ordered to "shoot to kill" but decided it'd had enough too and, yep, you guessed it—it was revolution time! The government was overthrown and Nicholas II gave up his throne (and was executed later in the year). When the temporary government didn't do much better, there was another revolution and this time a radical group called the Bolsheviks took power, with Vladimir Lenin in charge. He made peace with Germany, and Russia exited one war to fight another: a civil war of its own!

Did you know?

Rasputin had a huge beard and once went six months without changing his underwear, but he still had plenty of girlfriends. He survived several assassination attempts before he was finally killed by being poisoned, shot, and then thrown into a river for good measure!

It smells like someone in the room hasn't changed their underwear for six months!

That'll be our Rasputin. We think he's wonderful!

79 Brand-new Toys

World War I saw plenty of new weapons and technology used for the first time. Tanks were first used in 1916 and caused quite a shock. As recently as the start of the war, horses had been a common sight on the battlefield!

Thank goodness someone invented that thing! I'm fed up with pushing through mud, barbed wire and pot holes in this war!

Poison gas was an unwelcome addition to war weaponry, especially for the poor soldiers stuck in filthy trenches. When chlorine gas was first used by the Germans, there weren't any defenses in place. One piece of advice to protect yourself from gas was to put a urine-soaked cloth over your face!

Airships were a new way to travel, but the Germans soon realized that they were also a new way to fly to Britain and drop bombs! However, these airships, known as zeppelins, had one fatal flaw: they were full of hydrogen, which made

them float, but which is also very flammable. British pilots shot at the zeppelins with explosive ammunition and watched them burst into flames.

Submarines had actually already been used in the American Civil War, but the German submarines, called U-boats, were used to particularly devastating effect in World War I. The Germans didn't use them too cleverly, however, when they sank an American ship: this helped to prompt the Americans to enter the war in 1917.

Did you know?

Zeppelins were made from cow intestines: the Germans needed so many that making sausages was banned for a while!

The Roaring Twenties and Thrifty Thirties

The Years Between the World Wars

80 Super Suffragettes

Imagine living in a world where women weren't allowed to vote. Back at the turn of the 20th century, this was a reality in many countries, including Britain and the USA. Some brave women declared that they'd had quite enough and should have the same voting rights as men.

In Britain, Emmeline Pankhurst didn't think the politer methods of campaigning worked. She formed the Women's Social and Political Union (WSPU), whose members were called suffragettes. Emmeline's methods to get the vote for women were considered very unladylike indeed. She led protests in which vandalism and arson occurred, and which ended up with Emmeline and others being thrown in prison. They went on hunger strikes in jail, to which there was an unpleasant answer: force-feeding!

In 1908, Hyde Park in London was the sight of a rally of around half a million activists. Some of the female campaigners tied themselves to railings and smashed windows in Downing Street, the official residence of the Prime Minister, to get his attention. These women could look after themselves too. The suffragettes were trained in jujitsu for when things got nasty!

Finally, in 1928 after years of protests and violent clashes, all women over the age of 21 were given the right to vote in Britain. The USA was way ahead on this one—it gave women the vote in 1920. The first country to give woman the right to vote though was New Zealand, in 1893.

Did you know?

Emily Davison became one of the most famous suffragettes when she stepped out in front of the King's horse at the Epsom Derby in June 1913 and came to a very tragic end for her cause.

81 Roaring Twenties

The Roaring Twenties were a great time to be alive in the USA—at least for some people. The country experienced a real boom, with motor cars filling the roads and skyscrapers like the Empire State Building and the Chrysler Building in New York planned for construction.

Radio was the cool new form of entertainment, and jazz became the equivalent of today's pop music. People hit the dance floors, doing new moves with funny names like the Charleston and the Lindy Hop.

Some women started to dress in ways that fuddy-duddy old-timers didn't like, cutting their hair, wearing shorter skirts and makeup, and generally having a good time. These women were called "flappers."

The movies became popular, though they were mostly silent films (and you could forget about 3-D!).

The first talking movie, aptly called *The Jazz Singer*, showed at theaters in 1927. Spare a thought for some of the people living in the countryside, though—they often didn't enjoy the benefits the Roaring Twenties brought mainly to the cities.

Did you know?

Babe Ruth played baseball for the New York Yankees during the 1920s. He was quick on the baseball field, but he was even quicker behind the wheel. He was caught speeding doing 26 mph (42 kmh) and when they let him out of jail he sped straight to the stadium to play for the Yankees!

82 Al Capone

The Roaring Twenties coincided with Prohibition in the USA, which meant that alcohol was banned. People just ignored the ban and drank in illegal bars called "speakeasies;" and instead of the government making money from alcohol taxes, criminals made a fortune instead.

The most famous of these 1920s criminals was the Chicago gangster Al Capone. He was a new type of criminal who didn't shy away from publicity. He wore sharp suits and a diamond ring on his pinkie finger, and he would give huge tips to waiters. He was known as "Scarface" by the press, due to the scar he received in a gang fight when he was young. His crime operation was worth millions of dollars.

It didn't pay to be one of Al Capone's competitors, as he usually sorted them out with bullets. He famously had his men dress up as police to machine-gun an Irish gang called the North Side Gang on Valentine's Day in 1929, which really wasn't very romantic.

In all, he was linked to something like 400 murders—but what did he go to jail for? Not paying his taxes!

Did you know?

Al Capone was sent to Alcatraz, a maximum-security prison known as the "Rock," where he bribed his guards and lived a very easy life!

Hey guard! Fifty bucks for extra butter on my toast in the morning.

Sure thing Mr Capone! I'll even bring it to your cell with a coffee!

83 The Great Depression

The boom of the Roaring Twenties came to an abrupt halt with the Wall Street Crash of 1929, when the stock market lost billions of dollars. The Great Depression followed, in which millions of Americans lost their jobs and their homes. The USA then called in the loans it had made to European countries, so they all suffered a Great Depression of their own!

Prices fell so low in the USA that farmers left their crops and animals rotting in the fields because they weren't worth anything, but at the same time some people were in danger of starving. Something didn't quite add up there. Huge dust storms also hit the prairies, causing severe drought and leaving

the area a dust bowl: farming it was out of the question.

In cities, people queued for handouts of bread and soup to survive. Things were so bad that even Al Capone (before he went to jail) opened a soup kitchen to help! To help get the economy back on track, President Franklin D. Roosevelt put measures known as the New Deal in place, but, bizarrely, it was World War II and the resulting increase in American industry that lifted the country out of the Great Depression.

Did you know?

When news of the crash started spreading, some people rushed to the bank to take all their money out ... which only made things worse as it caused these banks to go bust!

War, What is it Good for? (Part 2)

World War II

84 Nasty Nazis

In 1933, Adolf Hitler, leader of the Nazi Party, came to power in Germany. He decided he rather liked power, so he banned all rival political parties!

With his horrible sidekicks Joseph Goebbels and Heinrich Himmler, Hitler made himself Führer (meaning "leader") and set about trying to make Germany powerful again. Or at least what powerful would look like in the eyes of a tyrannical

I like to get what I want.

madman. He invaded Poland to start World War II, and he used his secret police, the Gestapo, and some really bad guys called the SS to intimidate, torture, blackmail, and plant evidence to get the results he wanted.

The nasty Nazis burned books that they thought were unfit for Germany, such as those by Jewish scientist and genius Albert Einstein. (You might feel like doing that sometimes in the classroom, but this was really bad news!)

Hitler, Goebbels, and Himmler believed in the superiority of an Aryan "master race" of tall, blue-eyed, blond-haired people … despite the fact that none of these weasels fitted that description! This was terrible for anyone who didn't fit the mold (except for the Austrian-born Hitler and

My Führer. We don't fit any of the characteristics on our Aryan "master race" check list.

Shhh! Let's hope nobody notices!

his cronies, of course). Millions of people, particularly Jewish people, were sent to death camps and never seen again.

Did you know?

The Nazis were so bad that George Lucas definitely had them in mind when he created the evil Empire in the Star Wars movies, including Darth Vader's stormtroopers, who were named after a type of Nazi soldier also called storm troopers.

85 Winston Churchill

By May 1940, because of the actions of the Nazis, Europe was embroiled in all-out war again—World War II—and things were looking grim. Nazi Germany, led by Hitler, the mad monster with a mustache, was conquering Europe at a rapid rate, and Britain made Winston Churchill its Prime Minister. Soon, Britain and its colonies would stand alone against the Germans – at least until the USA and USSR got involved. Churchill's thoughts on the war were pretty clear. "We shall never surrender," he said, and he was as good as his word, though some people thought surrender seemed like a good idea!

Churchill had a real way with words, and his speeches helped the British keep their spirits up during the war. With his bow tie, hat, and cigars, and his "V for Victory" salute, he had an impressive air! Churchill managed Britain's war effort from

his underground
Cabinet War
Rooms in
London, which
were constructed
so German bombs
couldn't hit him.

When the Allies defeated
Germany in the war in
Europe, Churchill had his
most famous victory of all.
It was his last, because in the election that year in Britain
he lost and was given the boot as Prime Minister. That's
gratitude for you!

Did you know?

The Nazis had a cunning plan to kill Winston Churchill—using an exploding chocolate bar! Aiming at his appetite was a good idea, but British spies put a stop to it.

86 The Lightning War

The people in British cities during World War II dreaded the sound of air-raid sirens, because they knew it meant the German airplanes would soon be dropping bombs on them. They called these sirens "Moaning Minnies" because of the noise they made.

During the Blitz (which comes from "blitzkrieg", German for "lightning war"), the Germans really meant business. At one stage, they bombed London 57 nights in a row, and plenty of other British cities got it bad too. Gas masks were given out and air-raid shelters were built. People spent so much time in the shelters that they practically moved in!

In London, the underground Tube railway stations were used as air-raid shelters and thousands of people stayed in them. People traveling to work in the morning had to step over all the sleeping Londoners to get on their train!

Blackouts were ordered at night to make things harder for the bombers, so there were no lights on anywhere. Spooky!

Did you know?

A dog called Rip was a hero of the Blitz. He could sniff out people buried under rubble, saving over 100 lives and earning a medal for his trouble!

87 Waking Sleeping Giants

In December 1941, Japan did something really, really stupid. The USA was minding its own business and staying out of fighting in the war, while the Japanese were allied with Germany.

Tensions had been mounting between the USA and Japan, but nothing too serious ... until Japan made a sneaky surprise attack on the USA's Pearl Harbor base in Hawaii without declaring war first. Thousands of Americans were killed and injured, with ships damaged, and planes destroyed ... but it wasn't the knockout blow the Japanese had hoped for, because the USA promptly declared war on Japan. Then Germany and Italy stuck up for their pal Japan and declared war on the USA, so then the USA declared war back on them. So there!

The USA was now part of the Pacific War of World War II. After three years of warfare, it decided to use its devastating new weapon: the atomic bomb. It dropped one on the city of Hiroshima and another on Nagasaki, with catastrophic consequences for the people of Japan. The explosion wiped out 90 percent of the city and immediately killed 80,000 people; tens of thousands more later died of radiation exposure.

Did you know?

In 1974, some 29 years after the end of World War II, the last Japanese soldier surrendered. He had been hiding in the jungle on an island in the Philippines and thought the war was still going on!

I surrender! I surrender! 29 years in the jungle is enough for me!

Have I got news for you!

88 Rationing

The war at sea meant that enemy submarines and ships could stop supplies reaching both sides in the war. Food and materials were scarce, and countries including the USA, Australia, Britain, and Germany all suffered. People were given coupons that controlled how much butter, meat, sugar,

and tea could be bought, and even things like clothes were rationed. In Britain, rationing didn't stop until nine years after the war ended!

Things like bananas, which were grown far away, pretty much disappeared in Britain—someone managed to have an auction for a single banana and sold it for a whopping £5, which was more than some people earned in a week.

Britain also had something called the Ministry of Food, which printed advice in newspapers and produced films showing people how to stretch their rations further. They had one magic recipe for making a steak and kidney pie … without the steak and kidneys!

People were encouraged to grow their own vegetables, which the Ministry called "Digging for Victory." The Ministry used cartoons like "Potato Pete" and "Doctor Carrot" to appeal to

children, although they weren't always fooled! While you might not like to eat all your vegetables now, you might feel differently if there was nothing else to eat!

Did you know?

These carrots are faulty! I can't see a thing!

The idea that carrots can help you see in the dark started during World War II, as the British produced posters claiming it would help during the blackouts of the Blitz! Carrots contain vitamin A, and this is needed for your eyes to work in low-light conditions. If you have a vitamin A deficiency, you will develop night blindness. Eating carrots would correct this and improve your night vision, but only to the point of an ordinary healthy person.

89 Other Ways to Win Wars

Amazing airplanes like the German Messerschmitt and the British Spitfire fought in the sky, but there were less obvious ways to fight the war.

Propaganda played a big part. Many radio broadcasts, newspaper stories, posters, and even movies were used to lift the spirits of the population and trash-talk the enemy. Americans had posters with a strong woman called "Rosie

101 Cool Hilarious Histories

the Riveter" rolling up her sleeve saying, "We Can Do It!" and another saying, "Loose Lips Sink Ships," that warned gossiping soldiers and sailors to keep their mouths shut!

Movies played a part too, and Hollywood was busy making anti-Nazi films. The Germans had their own film industry, though one of their most famous actresses, Marlene Dietrich, had done the sensible thing and fled to Hollywood!

A bunch of super-smart people in Britain worked to crack the enemy codes so they could understand Germany's messages, which helped the Allies' ships avoid the dreaded German U-boats in the Atlantic Ocean.

> When you've cracked that secret U-Boat code Curuthers, let me know what it says.
>
> BRITS STINK

These geniuses even developed a very early form of computer for code-breaking called the Colossus—though you definitely couldn't play video games on this huge machine!

Did you know?

Nazi propaganda leaflets were targeted at British soldiers, "warning" them about their American allies: "They've got lots of money and loads of time to chase after your women!"

Reach for the Stars

1950s to 70s

90 Everest

Mount Everest is the highest mountain in the world, and has long held a fascination for climbers. British climber George Mallory was asked in 1924 why so many wanted to conquer it, and his answer was simple: "Because it's there." He disappeared on his way up the mountain and never came back, and people wondered if he made it to the top.

New Zealand climber Edmund Hillary and his Tibetan pal Tenzing Norgay made it to the top in 1953, and they have proof because they made it back alive! Well, that, and they took some photos looking down from the summit. They only spent 15 minutes up there before heading back down.

The climbers reached the top the day before the coronation of Queen Elizabeth II in Britain, which was a good excuse for a double celebration. The New Zealander was knighted and

became Sir Edmund Hillary, and Norgay was given the George Medal, as Nepalese citizens weren't eligible to be knighted.

Did you know?

In 1999, some 75 years after he disappeared, George Mallory's frozen body was finally found by a climbing expedition. The hobnail boots and state-of-the-art 1920s climbing gear were a giveaway ... but had he made it to the top and been on his way down or was he still climbing up?

91 Elvis

Put simply, Elvis Presley was "the King of Rock 'n' Roll." With his good looks and slick hair, he announced himself to the world in the 1950s. His snake-like hip shaking might look tame by today's standards, but back then adults were shocked, calling it "obscene." It was demanded that he should only be

filmed from the waist up, to keep those snaky hips from the country's TV screens. The kids, naturally, loved it!

He had number one records (yes, records—there was no downloading or streaming then), bought himself a mansion with an indoor waterfall, and became a movie star too. Elvis had it all! Or at least so it seemed …

He was drafted into the army where he served like any normal soldier. When he eventually grew tired of Hollywood, Elvis made a great comeback to music and television in 1968 and he started wearing his distinctive jumpsuits. By the 1970s, however, the unthinkable happened for to the idolized star: he was eating way too much and he got really big! Sadly, in 1977, at just 42 years old, he was found dead in his bathroom, having collapsed on the toilet.

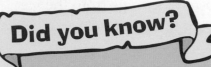

Did you know?

Elvis's favorite treat was a Fool's Gold Loaf, which was a hollowed-out loaf of bread filled with a whole jar of peanut butter, a jar of jelly, and a pound of bacon. He once traveled in his private jet just to pick one up!

92 Castro's Cuba

Fidel Castro and Ernesto "Che" Guevara led the Cuban Revolution and in 1959 they overthrew President Batista, the country's dictator. Castro and Guevara were both heroes to their people, and Guevara became so famous that college students all over the world wore T-shirts with his face on them to show that they too were revolutionaries (at heart).

Fidel loved cigars and communism and he hated the USA. The feeling was mutual, as the US was worried about Fidel's friendship with the Soviet Union (also known as the USSR: what is largely modern-day Russia). There were 634 attempts to assassinate him, mainly by the CIA, and he survived them all! That's probably not surprising once you hear what some of them were. One plot was to give him an exploding cigar, while another involved a wet suit with poison in it. The CIA even toyed with the idea of using a powder that would make his beard fall out, which they hoped would make him less popular. They might have been getting desperate at this stage!

Did you know?

Fidel Castro created the world record for the longest speech ever given at the United Nations, at 4 hours and 29 minutes long.

93 The MAD Arms Race

The USA and USSR took part in an arms race and by the 1960s, each side had enough nuclear weapons to completely wipe the other one out. This was called "mutually assured destruction," or the aptly named "MAD" for short! You'd have to be mad

to fire them, because the return fire from the enemy would basically mean the end of both sides.

But that almost didn't stop things coming to a head during the Cuban Missile Crisis in 1962. After the disastrous Bay of Pigs attack, when the CIA sponsored an invasion of Cuba, the Cubans understandably felt a bit nervous about another attack from their neighbor, so they asked the Soviet Union if it wouldn't mind setting up some nuclear-missile sites as protection. The USSR was happy to oblige!

A standoff followed: the Americans blocked Soviet ships from bringing weapons into Cuba, which annoyed the Soviet Union as the US had missiles in countries neighboring the USSR. Things got so tense that it looked like World War III was a real possibility. Eventually though, a compromise was reached, and the world let out a huge sigh of relief. Phew!

Did you know?

When an American destroyer dropped depth charges on a Soviet submarine during the crisis, the Soviet captain gave the order to fire a nuclear weapon. Thankfully, another officer refused and suggested going up to the surface to check whether World War III had actually started before firing!

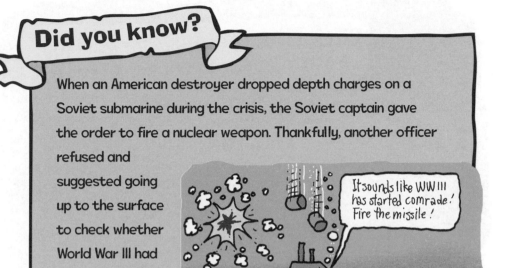

94 Space Race

In the 1950s and 60s, the Americans and the Russians were like two gangs of overly competitive kids. They didn't just have an arms race with each other—they also had a space race!

The Soviet Union took an early lead. In 1957, it launched the first satellite into orbit, called Sputnik 1. They spectacularly followed that up in 1961, when Soviet pilot Yuri Gagarin became the first man in space. He was there for less than two hours, but it certainly counts!

The USA was a little upset by all this, and needed to catch up. President John F. Kennedy made a speech claiming that America would land a man on the moon before the decade was over.

He was right, but Kennedy didn't live to see it, as he was assassinated in 1963. In 1969, American astronaut Neil Armstrong became the first man to set foot on the moon, uttering the immortal line: "That's one small step for man, one giant leap for mankind." His pal Buzz Aldrin followed him, but, just like the Soviet Union, he found there were no prizes for second place in the space race!

Their return journey was almost a disaster though! Neil Armstrong and Buzz Aldrin returned to the Lunar Module,

only to realise that a switch on a crucial circuit breaker had broken. This particular broken switch left them without a way to ignite the engine to get back home to earth! NASA tried to find a way to repair it but weren't having any success. Eventually, Aldrin decided to just shove his pen into the mechanism, creating a makeshift switch. Surprisingly, and thankfully, it worked and the astronauts made it home.

Did you know?

Laika the dog beat all of humanity to space: she became the first animal to go into orbit in 1957. An early victory for the Soviet Union!

95   The Beatles

John, Paul, George, and Ringo were the Beatles: four young men from Liverpool in England who changed the world of pop music.

They were the first proper "boy band," with their mop-top hair and all the screaming girls that come with being in a band! This frenzy became known as Beatlemania, and it was so intense that the band sometimes feared for their own safety. The screaming was so bad that no one could actually hear the music, so they basically stopped playing live in 1966.

The Beatles weren't like boy bands today though: they actually played instruments! They also wrote their own songs, the likes of which had never been heard before. They went to India to expand their minds, and it certainly did that, as they ditched the mop-top look, grew long hair and beards, and wore psychedelic outfits. They had a message of peace and love, which young people loved.

The Beatles did play live again: their last-ever concert was on a rooftop in central London, with people on the street and other rooftops watching on in amazement. The police turned up, but they just stood and watched too for over 40 minutes!

Did you know?

When one of the Beatles, John Lennon, married Yoko Ono in 1969, they spent a week doing a "bed-in" (instead of a sit-in) protest for world peace, where they spent a week in bed in their hotel room and journalists and photographers visited them!

96 Martin Luther King Jr

Martin Luther King Jr had a dream—that black Americans could be treated as equals with white Americans—and it was a dream he hoped to achieve peacefully.

In 1955 in the city of Montgomery, Alabama, there was a system of segregation on buses: white people sat at the front and black people had to sit at the back. When Rosa Parks, a black woman, refused to give up her seat for a white man, she was arrested, so Martin Luther King led black people in a boycott of the city's buses that lasted for 381 days. That's a lot of walking to work and school! It was worth it, as they won in the end, and segregation was scrapped.

Protests started kicking off all around the country. Black people started a "sit-in" movement: they went to places that were segregated, like a lunch counter, sat in the white section,

and refused to leave, no matter what abuse or even violence came their way! In 1963, King led a march on Washington, D.C. of 250,000 people, and gave one of his most inspiring speeches. Eventually, after a struggle filled with arrests, hurt, and threats against them, a legal, if not necessarily real, equality was achieved. Black people were allowed to vote—a long time after white women won that right.

Did you know?

Martin's enemies didn't share his peaceful approach, and in 1968 he was tragically shot. Some 10 years earlier he'd been stabbed with a letter opener, and was told afterwards that if he'd sneezed, it would have killed him!

97 Muhammad Ali

Muhammad Ali was the boxer who could "float like a butterfly and sting like a bee." He wasn't called "the Greatest" for nothing, and he wasn't always called Muhammad Ali, either.

When he started boxing, he was called Cassius Clay, and he soon became known for his sharp tongue as well as his fighting skills. He won the world title and told the world: "I am the prettiest thing that ever lived!" When he converted to Islam, he changed his name to Muhammad Ali.

When Ali refused to fight in the Vietnam War, he said what was on the minds of many Americans at the time: "Man, I ain't got no quarrel with them Viet Cong." But a lot of white people

in America didn't like this: they took his championships away and banned him from boxing for several years!

When he made a comeback in the 1970s, Ali wasn't quite as sharp—but he was still the Greatest. No one thought he had a chance in 1974 for the "Rumble in the Jungle": a world heavyweight championship bout that took place in Zaire (now the Democratic Republic of Congo). Ali fought the man-mountain (and later grill-maker!) George Foreman in one of the most famous boxing matches ever. But Ali used his famous "rope-a-dope" tactic (pretending to be trapped against the ropes, leading an opponent to throw tiring and ineffective punches) before knocking Foreman out.

Did you know?

Among the many Ali boasts was this: "I'm so fast that last night I turned off the light switch in my hotel room and got into bed before the room was dark."

Modern Marvels

1980s to today

98 Berlin Wall

After World War II, Germany was divided into East Germany and West Germany, with Britain, France, and the USA taking control of the west, and the Soviet Union taking control of the east. These powers divided Berlin in the same way, despite it technically being in the Soviet Union's territory. The result was two countries, East and West Germany, and a politically divided Berlin (located in East Germany).

The way of life enforced by the Soviet Union, with stricter rules and a tough police force, made West Germany seem a more

attractive option for many East Germans. To stop people leaving, one night in 1961 the Soviet Union quickly and secretly put up a wall around the whole of West Berlin! Some people woke up trapped on the wrong side of the city. The wall was just a barbed-wire fence to start with, but eventually it became a concrete wall with armed guards to stop people crossing. People were shot if they dared to try.

On November 9, 1989, with the Cold War at last beginning to thaw, free movement was once again allowed, and millions of people crossed the border, drinking champagne, hammering off bits of the wall, and celebrating. But the biggest celebration was yet to come: on New Year's Eve, TV-star-turned-singer David Hasselhoff performed his hit single "Looking for Freedom" on the wall. This song became the soundtrack to the reunification of the country, despite it not being much of a hit elsewhere!

Did you know?

There was a bright side to the Berlin Wall for one group of people: graffiti artists. It was a huge blank canvas for those on the west side of the wall to paint on. Some of this art has been preserved and can still be seen today.

99 Home Computers

It wasn't until the 1970s that owning a computer in the home became a realistic ambition, and even then, the computers didn't look anything like those we use today!

In 1977, a certain company you may have heard of called Apple released its Apple II home computer, and it was a real game changer … once it was plugged into a television set! Apple sold millions of these computers.

Steve Jobs founded Apple, along with Steve Wozniak. Jobs was happy to work with a young man called Bill Gates, whose Microsoft company made software, until Gates produced the first version of Windows in 1983 and Jobs accused him of ripping off Apple! And so began a fierce rivalry between the

two, where Jobs would say things like, "The only problem with Microsoft is they just have no taste." That, however, didn't stop Apple from gratefully receiving a $150 million bailout from Microsoft in 1997!

There was competition on a more modest scale between Clive Sinclair (Sinclair Research) and Christopher Curry (Acorn Computers), who were based in Britain's answer to Silicon Valley—leafy Cambridge! When Sinclair took exception to an advertisement Curry had taken out in a local newspaper, he found Curry in a pub and attacked him with the rolled-up newspaper. Ow!

Did you know?

He might have been the man behind the iPod and the iPhone, but that doesn't mean Steve Jobs didn't have some odd habits! He used to soak his feet in the toilet to relieve stress, he nearly named the Apple Macintosh computer the Apple Bicycle, and he once wanted his factory to be bright blue so he had all the machines painted ... which broke them!

100 Nelson Mandela

Nelson Mandela was the first black president in South Africa after the country got rid of its awful apartheid system, which segregated white and black people. The election Mandela won in 1994 was the first one that black people were even allowed to vote!

When he was young, Mandela trained as a lawyer and wanted to challenge apartheid peacefully, but when 69 black people were massacred by police in 1960, he decided he'd given peace a chance and it was time to explore other options.

He was eventually arrested and given a life sentence for sabotage against the government in 1964, and he spent 27 years in prison. While he was there, however, people around the world campaigned for his release, and lots of sports teams refused to play in South Africa as a protest against apartheid.

When apartheid was finally scrapped, Mandela was freed and eventually became president. It was time to give peace a chance. With sports teams now happy to play there, South Africa hosted the Rugby World Cup in 1995 and Mandela got his fairytale ending, standing on the winners' podium proudly wearing his South African jersey.

Did you know?

Nelson Mandela was only removed from the USA's terrorist watch list in 2008—when he was 89! We can't imagine the threat they imagined he still posed.

101 Y2K

By the end of the 1990s, technology had advanced in leaps and bounds. Computers were in many homes, cell phones (now called "mobiles") had progressed from the huge brick-sized devices of the 1980s to actually fit in a pocket, and Tim Berners-Lee's invention, a little something called the World Wide Web, meant the Internet was now a reality for everyone, even if Wi-Fi was still a way off yet!

But when the clocks passed midnight on New Year's Eve at the end of 1999, one technological threat was believed to have the potential to derail the whole of civilization: the Millennium Bug. Some vital computer systems were written by programmers who hadn't bothered using the whole year in

their code and just used the last two digits (such as 00 for the year 2000). This meant computers wouldn't be able to tell the year 2000 from a year like 1900.

Governments spent millions fixing the bug, fearful that computers would go haywire and cause planes to fall out of the sky or power plants to fail. Some even feared it meant nuclear war and THE END OF THE WORLD!

When New Year's Eve 1999 came around, some people hid in bunkers expecting the apocalypse while others partied the night away. But when the clocks passed midnight ... everything was fine: there was another century packed full of hilarious histories to come!

Did you know?

On the 17th we need to take the dog to the vet. On the 20th it's dinner with the Jonses and the 21st is the end of the world.

People only had to wait 12 years for another opportunity to worry about the end of the world. A number of people believed that the ancient Mayan calendar pointed to an apocalypse on December 21, 2012, and so the world waited. False alarm (again)!

The History of the Future

Predictions of Things to Come

History is made by people: people just like you, your family, your friends, and yes, even your teachers! And when you think about it, we're making history now, every day: as we live our lives and make our choices. Who knows what effect doing your homework or cleaning your room (or not …) might have?

Predictions of Things to Come

Over the course of human history, the only constant has been change. That makes it very hard to guess what will happen in the future. But did you know that there are people called "futurists," whose job it is to try to predict what will come? Some of their predictions include:

 3-D printers will make everything from clothes and houses to human organs and even food!

 We'll be able to live in a virtual world thanks to nanobots (microscopic robots) in our brains. Nanobots will also be able to cure diseases.

 People will be able to read other people's minds, or at least experience their emotions and feelings, through computer interfaces. You might even be able to buy emotions!

 We'll be able to understand other languages using universal translators.

 People will fly in rockets to space hotels orbiting the Earth or the moon.

 Automated drones will do everything from delivering parcels to monitoring forest fires.

Artificial intelligence will be used in medicine and surgery, cars, and even our clothes. We already have driverless cars, though they are not yet fully autonomous. One day soon, people predict, they'll be the normal form of car transportation!

Of course, these are just predictions: who knows what will really happen!? People a hundred years or so ago wouldn't recognize the world today, but they did predict space travel, home computers, earphones, the Internet, Wi-Fi, nuclear power and the atomic bomb, mobile phones, television, and much more. Mind you, there were also less successful predictions, such as the extinction of cockroaches, flies, and mosquitoes, the removal of C, Q, and X from the alphabet, that high-speed rail wouldn't happen because passengers wouldn't be able to breathe, and that rock music and bands like the Beatles wouldn't be successful!

Predictions of Things to Come

Perhaps the best way to predict the future is to wait and see, and instead do our best to create an interesting, worthwhile, and fun present for those future students who will have to study us as history!